AS/A-LEVEL YEAR 1

STUDENT GUIDE

AQA

Psychology

Introductory topics in psychology (includes psychopathology)

Social influence

Memory

Attachment

Psychopathology

Molly Marshall

PHILIP ALLAN FOR
HODDER
EDUCATION
AN HACHETTE UK COMPANY

Philip Allan, an imprint of Hodder Education, an Hachette UK company, Blenheim Court, George Street, Banbury, Oxfordshire OX16 5BH.

Orders

Bookpoint Ltd, 130 Milton Park, Abingdon, Oxfordshire OX14 4SB

tel: 01235 827827

fax: 01235 400401

e-mail: education@bookpoint.co.uk

Lines are open 9.00 a.m.–5.00 p.m., Monday to Saturday, with a 24-hour message answering service. You can also order through the Hodder Education website: www.hoddereducation.co.uk

© Molly Marshall 2015

ISBN 978-1-4718-4372-3

First printed 2015

Impression number 5 4 3 2 1

Year 2018 2017 2016 2015

This guide has been written specifically to support students preparing for the AQA AS and A-level Psychology examinations. The content has been neither approved nor endorsed by AQA and remains the sole responsibility of the author.

Typeset by Integra Software Services Pvt. Ltd., Pondicherry, India

Printed in Italy

Hachette UK's policy is to use papers that are natural, renewable and recyclable products and made from wood grown in sustainable forests. The logging and manufacturing processes are expected to conform to the environmental regulations of the country of origin.

Contents

Content Guidance

Questions & Answers

■ Getting the most from this book

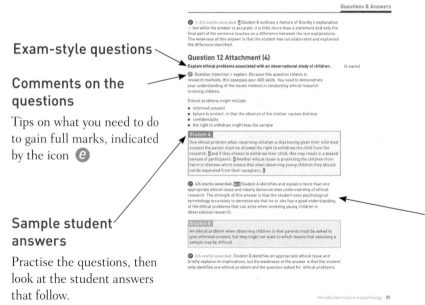

Exam-style questions

Comments on the questions

Tips on what you need to do to gain full marks, indicated by the icon **e**

Sample student answers

Practise the questions, then look at the student answers that follow.

Commentary on sample student answers

Find out how many marks each answer would be awarded in the exam and then read the comments (preceded by the icon **e**) following each student answer. Annotations that link back to points made in the student answers show exactly how and where marks are gained or lost.

■ About this book

This is a guide to the topics of **social influence**, **memory** and **attachment** which are examined on A-level and AS Paper 1, and to **psychopathology** which is examined on A-level Paper 1, and AS Paper 2. The guide is intended as a revision aid rather than as a textbook. It focuses on how the specification content is examined and how different answers to sample questions may be assessed.

For each of the topics — social influence, memory, attachment and psychopathology — the following are provided:

- appropriate content relevant to each topic. This is not intended as the *only* appropriate content for a given topic, but gives you an idea of what you might include and how you might present an answer to a question set on a particular aspect of the specification
- a glossary of key terms, constructed to be succinct but informative
- example questions in the style of AQA A-level and AS examination questions, together with full explanations of their requirements as well as the appropriate breakdown of marks between AO1, AO2 and AO3 skills
- an example grade A/B and C/D response to each of these questions, with comments showing where marks have been gained or lost

Specification

The topics in this book are examined on the AS and A-level papers outlined in the table below.

Topic	AS	A-level
Social influence	Paper 1	Paper 1
Memory	Paper 1	Paper 1
Attachment	Paper 1	Paper 1
Psychopathology	Paper 2	Paper 1

How to use this guide

This guide is not intended to provide a set of model answers to possible examination questions, or an account of the right material to include in any examination question. It is intended to give you an idea of how your examination will be structured and how you might improve your examination performance.

You should read through the relevant topic in the Content Guidance section before you attempt a question from the Questions & Answers section. Look at the sample answers only after you have tackled the question yourself.

Content Guidance

This section gives content guidance on the topics of social influence, memory, attachment and psychopathology. Each topic contains information on the theories and studies that comprise the specification content. Knowledge of appropriate theories, studies and research methods is essential for the examination. It is also important to be able to assess the value of these theories, studies and research methods.

At the end of each topic, a glossary of key terms is provided — those terms that you will need to use, or may be asked to define, in an examination.

Author names and publication dates have been given when referring to research studies. The full references for these studies should be available in textbooks if you wish to research the topic further.

■ Social influence

This topic is examined on AS Paper 1 and on A-level Paper 1.

Social psychology focuses on how we interact with other people and how these interactions may influence our own behaviour. You need to understand how psychologists have defined social influence, psychological explanations of why people may or may not yield to majority influence (conformity), the influence of social roles and the processes involved in obedience, as well as the processes involved in minority influence and social change.

Types of conformity

- **Internalisation.** This occurs when an individual conforms because he or she believes that a group norm for behaviour or a group attitude is 'right'. If group pressure is removed, this conformity will continue.
- **Identification.** This occurs when an individual conforms to the role that society expects him or her to play. The individual does not have to change his or her private opinion. An example is the study by Zimbardo.
- **Compliance.** This occurs when a person conforms to the majority opinion but does not agree with it. If group pressure is removed, the conformity will cease. Compliance is thought to occur because an individual wishes to be accepted by the majority group.
- **Majority influence (conformity).** This is the process that takes place when an individual's attitudes or behaviour are affected by the views of the dominant group. This may be because of **normative social influence** (the effect of social norms), but can also occur because of **informational social influence** when the minority yields to group pressure because they think that the majority has more knowledge or information.

- **Informational social influence.** This occurs when a question asked does not have an obviously correct answer. When this happens, people look to others for information and may agree with the majority view. Informational social influence involves the process of **compliance**. An example is the study by Sherif.
- **Normative social influence.** This occurs when an individual agrees with the opinions of a group of people because he or she wishes to be accepted by them. The influenced individual may not change his or her private belief. An example is the study by Asch.
- **Minority influence.** This is the process that takes place when a consistent minority changes the attitudes and/or behaviour of an individual. Social psychologists propose that it is the consistency of the minority that is important since it demonstrates a firm, alternative view to that of the majority. Minority influence leads to a change in attitudes and involves the process of conversion.

Explanations for conformity

Conformity as the result of informational social influence (Sherif 1935)

Aim: To measure informational social influence.

Procedures: Participants were shown a still point of light in a dark room. In this situation, an optical illusion called the autokinetic effect occurs, when the point of light appears to move. The participants were asked to estimate how far the point of light had moved, first as individuals, then in a group, and finally as individuals again.

Findings: In the group estimate condition, participants changed their personal estimate and a group norm emerged. This norm was reflected in their final individual estimates.

Conclusion: Since there was no 'factually correct answer', the group norm emerged because individuals looked to others for information. Informational social influence involves **internalisation** when an individual conforms because he or she believes that a group norm or opinion is 'right'. If group pressure is removed, this conformity will continue.

Conformity as the result of normative social influence (Asch 1956)

Aim: To measure the effect of normative social influence.

Procedures: In a laboratory experiment that used a repeated measures design, groups of seven or eight male students were shown a stimulus line (S) and then three other lines (A, B and C). There was only one 'real' participant in each group. The others were confederates who were helping the experimenter. All the participants were asked to say out loud which line (A, B or C) matched the stimulus line. The real participant always answered last or last but one. Each participant completed 18 trials, and in 12 of the trials (the critical trials), the confederates had all been primed to give the same wrong answer. ➜

Findings: In the control trials, the real participants gave incorrect answers 0.7% of the time. In the critical trials, they gave incorrect answers that conformed to the majority view 37% of the time. Of the real participants, 75% conformed at least once. After the experiment, the real participants were asked why they answered as they had. Some said that they did not believe the answers given by the others in the group but they had not wanted to look different.

Conclusion: Normative social influence had taken place — the real participants agreed with the opinion of the group because they wished to be accepted by them. This demonstrated that participants gave wrong answers because of compliance rather than conversion. **Compliance** occurs when a person conforms to the majority opinion in public but in private does not agree. If group pressure is removed, the conformity will cease. Compliance is thought to occur because an individual wishes to be accepted by the majority group.

Exam tip

An exam question might describe a hypothetical social situation and then ask you to identify what type of conformity is likely to occur. Make sure you can define both normative and informational social influence.

Evaluation

Sherif (1935)

- **Limitations.** Assessing how far a spot of light has moved is a trivial task and not one that is likely to happen in everyday life. The study has low mundane validity — people may be less likely to be influenced by others in real-life situations.

Asch (1956)

- **Strengths.** The experimental method leads to meaningful results because there is control over variables. Statements can be made about cause and effect. The study can be replicated.
- **Limitations.** The biased sample of male American students may not be representative of other populations. The study has low mundane validity; it does not represent a lifelike social situation. People may not change their opinions about social variables as readily as they do about line lengths. The study was unethical because Asch deceived the participants.

Knowledge check 1

In social influence research, what is meant by compliance?

Conformity to social roles

Zimbardo et al. (1973)

Background: There had been a series of violent prison riots in America, and one explanation for this behaviour was that both prisoners and guards have personalities that make conflict inevitable — prisoners lack respect for authority and guards are attracted to the job because of a desire for power. This is a dispositional hypothesis and it suggests that both prisoners and guards are inevitably 'evil'. Zimbardo suggested that it was possible to separate the effects of the prison environment from the personalities of the inhabitants to test the dispositional hypothesis. →

Aims: To investigate conformity to social roles and to find out whether conformity is caused by the characteristics of the person (dispositional characteristics), or because of the situation he or she is in (situational factors).

Procedures: An advertisement sought male volunteers, to be paid $15 a day, for a study of 'prison life'. The 24 most stable men (physically and mentally) were selected from 75 volunteers. Participants were randomly assigned to the role of either a prisoner or a guard. There were two reserves and one person dropped out, so in the end there were 10 prisoners and 11 guards, all students, and largely middle class. A mock prison was built in the basement of Stanford University. It had three small cells equipped with a cot for each prisoner, a solitary confinement cell, various rooms for the guards and an interview room. There was also an indoor 'yard' with an observation screen at one end for video-recording equipment and space for observers.

The prisoners remained in prison throughout the study. The guards worked three-man, 8-hour shifts and were each given a uniform, a whistle, a wooden baton and sunglasses. They were told that they should 'maintain a reasonable degree of order within the prison' but were given no further instructions about how to behave. The prisoners were told to be at home on a particular Sunday. They were 'arrested', booked and fingerprinted and were then blindfolded and driven to the prison. There, they were stripped, deloused and issued with prison uniform: a numbered smock, a light ankle chain, rubber sandals and a cap to make it look as though their hair had been cut off. They were not allowed personal belongings in their cells but were allowed certain 'rights': three meals a day, three supervised toilet trips, 2 hours for reading or letter-writing, and two visiting periods and movies per week. They had to line up three times a day to be counted and tested on the prison rules. The guards only referred to the prisoners by number.

Findings: The prison environment had a huge impact on the feelings and behaviour of all participants. The guards became sadistic and oppressive. They increased the length of the line-ups until some of them lasted several hours. They decided that the prisoners should only receive their rights as a privilege, in return for good behaviour, and some guards volunteered to do extra hours without pay. Punishments included solitary confinement and humiliation. The prisoners, after short-lived resistance, became passive and depressed. Some prisoners coped by becoming sick, whereas others coped by being obedient. Five prisoners had to be released early because of extreme depression (crying, rage and acute anxiety). These symptoms had started to appear within 2 days. The experiment was ended after 6 days, despite the intention to continue for 2 weeks. Even when participants believed they were unobserved, they conformed to their roles.

Conclusions: There was strong evidence of conformity to social roles for prisoners and guards. Afterwards, participants reported that they had 'acted out of character', and there was no lasting change in their private opinions. The conformity was due to the social situation rather than to the personal characteristics of the male student participants. Zimbardo suggested that three processes could explain the prisoners' 'submission':

- **Deindividuation:** the prisoners lost their sense of individuality.
- **Learned helplessness:** the unpredictable decisions of the guards led the prisoners to give up responding.
- **Dependency:** the fact that the prisoners depended on the guards for everything emasculated the men and increased their sense of helplessness.

Identification occurs when an individual conforms to the role that society expects them to play. Both guards and prisoners identified with and conformed to the roles they had been allocated.

Evaluation

Zimbardo et al. (1973)
- **Strengths.** This research is useful as it can be applied to improve the situation in real prisons, e.g. by training guards to treat prisoners differently.
- **Limitations.** The artificial situation may have led to demand characteristics. The guards and prisoners may have been acting rather than conforming to their roles. It is possible that media stereotypes of aggressiveness may have influenced the guards' behaviour. Thus the study may not have been a valid measure of conformity to social roles. The prisoners and guards were all young and about the same age. A real prison is an established social community and the prisoners do not all arrive at the same time, so the sample did not represent the population of a real prison.

Obedience and conformity: the differences

Obedience
- Obedience occurs within a social hierarchy.
- The emphasis is on social power.
- The obedient behaviour is often different from the behaviour of the authority figure.
- The motivation for behaviour is explicit.
- Participants explain their behaviour in terms of obedience.

Conformity
- Conformity occurs between people of equal status.
- The emphasis is on social acceptance.
- The conformist behaviour is the same as that of the social group.
- The motivation for behaviour is implicit.
- Participants often deny their behaviour is motivated by conformity.

Exam tip

In an exam you might be asked to explain why the prisoners and guards conformed to their allocated roles. Make sure you can explain the psychological processes involved.

Knowledge check 2

Outline evidence that suggests both the prisoners and the guards conformed to their social roles.

Explanations for obedience

Research into obedience (Milgram 1963)

Milgram points out that obedience can explain some of the worst examples of human behaviour and that it is a commonly observed social fact that 'the individual who is commanded by a legitimate authority ordinarily obeys'.

Aims: Milgram wanted to find out why people obey authority when they are requested to do something unreasonable, what conditions foster obedient behaviour and what conditions foster independent behaviour.

Procedures: Milgram advertised, using a newspaper and direct mailing, for men to take part in a study of memory and learning at Yale University. Everyone was paid $4 for coming to the laboratory and they were told that the payment did not depend on remaining in the study for its duration. The chosen participants were 40 men aged between 20 and 50 who came from various occupational backgrounds.

There were two further participants: the experimenter was a biology teacher, and the learner (Mr Wallace) was a 47-year-old accountant. Both were confederates of Milgram. The participants were deceived about the purpose of the research. They were told that the aim of the experiment was to see how punishment affected learning. The naïve participant was paired with the confederate and both drew lots to see who would play the part of the 'teacher' and who would be the 'learner'. The confederate always got the part of the learner. The learner was strapped into a chair in the next room attached to an electrode. He was to listen to a list of word pairs and then be given one word and a choice of four possible answers. He was asked to say which of the four was correct. Every time the learner got a question wrong, the teacher would administer an electric shock and the shocks increased in voltage with each mistake. The teacher could see the shock levels displayed on the machine.

The teacher was given a slight shock of 45 volts as a demonstration that the machine was working, but in actuality no other real shocks were given. For the rest of the time, the learner pretended to be receiving shocks. In the experiment, the learner mainly gave wrong answers and for each of these the teacher gave him an electric shock. When the shocks reached 300 volts, the learner pounded on the wall and then gave no response to the next question. When the teacher asked the experimenter for guidance, the experimenter gave the standard instruction, 'an absence of response should be treated as a wrong answer'. After the 315-volt shock, the learner pounded on the wall again but after that, the learner made no other response. If at any time the teacher said he wished to stop, the experimenter used a sequence of four standard 'prods', which were repeated if necessary:

Prod 1: Please continue.

Prod 2: The experiment requires that you continue.

Prod 3: It is absolutely essential that you continue.

Prod 4: You have no other choice, you must go on.

If the teacher asked whether the learner might suffer permanent physical injury, the experimenter said, 'Although the shocks may be painful, there is no permanent tissue damage, so please go on.' If the teacher said that the learner clearly wanted to stop, the experimenter said, 'Whether the learner likes it or not, you must go on until he has learned all the word pairs correctly. So please go on.'

The key findings:

■ Twenty-six of the 40 participants (65%) went all the way to 450 volts with the electric shocks.

■ Only nine participants (22.5%) stopped at 315 volts.

Other findings: Before the study Milgram had asked 14 psychology students to predict how participants would behave, and the students had estimated that no more than 3% of the participants would continue to 450 volts. People who observed through one-way mirrors were astonished at the participants' behaviour.

The participants showed signs of extreme tension: most of them were observed to 'sweat, tremble, stutter, bite their lips, groan and dig their finger-nails into their flesh', and quite a few laughed nervously.

At the end of the study, all the participants were debriefed. They were reunited with the victim, assured there had been no real shocks and told that their behaviour was normal. They were also sent a follow-up questionnaire which showed that 84% felt glad to have participated, and 74% felt they had learned something of personal importance. Only one person reported that he felt sorry to have participated.

Knowledge check 4

List one quantitative and one qualitative finding from the Milgram study.

Variations on Milgram's original experiment

The change factors and percentages who obeyed were:

■ Experimenter instructed teacher by telephone (distance order); 23% obedience.

■ Experiment moved from Yale to a scruffy office (less prestige in location); 48% obedience.

■ Teacher was in the same room as the learner (increased proximity); 40% obedience.

■ Other teachers refused to give shocks (social support in refusal); 10% obedience.

■ Two teachers, one told by other to give shocks (reduced responsibility); 92.5% obedience.

■ Female participants; 65% obedience.

■ Experimenter was a member of the public (reduced authority); 20% obedience.

Conclusions

Milgram concluded that ordinary people will obey orders, in conflict with their conscience, even if this means harming someone else, but that situational factors may determine how people will behave:

■ **Legitimate authority.** If the person giving the order has legitimate authority, people transfer the responsibility for their actions to the authority figure.

■ **Agentic state.** People act as agents of the legitimate authority and hold the authority figure responsible for their actions.

■ **The slippery slope.** People follow a small 'reasonable' order and then feel obliged to continue when the orders gradually become unreasonable.

In the exam be prepared to give two reasons why the participants in the Milgram study obeyed, and apply this to everyday situations — for example, why you might obey your teacher in the classroom but not if you meet him/her outside school.

Evaluation

Strengths

- Milgram's experiment increased the understanding of obedience and the dangers of obedience.
- It made obvious the power relationships between authority figures and those they command.
- Most participants said they were glad they had taken part because they learned something of personal importance.
- The participants did believe they were giving shocks (high experimental realism).

Limitations

- There was a lack of informed consent, participants were deceived, and their right to withdraw was breached (though it could be argued that participants could have chosen to leave), which caused stress.
- The sample was biased as they were all male volunteers.
- The task had low external validity because the task did not reflect one that would occur in real life: teachers do not give shocks to students who give wrong answers.
- The experiment may have changed the way participants saw themselves and damaged their self-esteem.

Exam tip

When you evaluate the Milgram study, rather than making trite comments about a lack of ecological validity, focus on why the situation seemed to be 'realistic' to the participants.

Situational variables affecting obedience

Research into obedience in real-life situations

Hofling et al. (1966)

Aim: To study obedience in a real-life setting.

Procedures: Twenty-two nurses working in a hospital were telephoned by an unknown doctor and asked to administer a drug to a patient. The doctor said he would sign the required paperwork later. To obey, the nurses would have to break hospital rules not to take telephone instructions and not to administer drugs unless the paperwork was completed. The dosage instruction was twice the maximum recommended on the drug label.

Findings: Twenty-one nurses obeyed the doctor and would have administered the drug had they not been stopped. The nurses said that they were often given instructions over the telephone and that doctors were annoyed if they refused.

Conclusion: This was a real-life setting in which doctors had high prestige, legitimate authority and power over nurses, and obedience to authority was high.

Exam tip

Make sure you can identify the reasons why the nurses obeyed the doctor.

Meeus and Raaijmakers (1995)

Aim: To study obedience in a real-life setting in Holland.

Procedures: At a time of high unemployment in Holland, 24 participants were asked to conduct interviews to test how 'potential job applicants' responded to stress (the job applicants were in fact trained confederates). The participants were prompted to deliver 15 stressful remarks (e.g. this job is too difficult for you), designed to cause increasing levels of psychological distress. It was assumed that participants would, when they saw the distress they were causing, refuse to continue. The confederates started out by acting in a confident manner but then showed distress and eventually begged the interviewer to stop.

Findings: In spite of seeing the visible distress they were causing, 22 of the 24 participants delivered all 15 stress-causing remarks.

Conclusion: In this realistic face-to-face situation, most participants were obedient and were prepared to cause psychological harm.

Dispositional explanations for obedience

The authoritarian personality

The authoritarian personality is a theory devised in the 1950s to explain the events that led to the killing of 6 million Jews in Germany in the Second World War. The theory includes the Adorno F-scale (F for Fascist), which supposedly measures Fascist tendencies by evaluating responses to a series of weighted questions. According to Adorno's theory, some of the elements of the authoritarian personality type are:

- blind allegiance to conventional beliefs about right and wrong
- respect for submission to acknowledged authority
- belief in aggression toward those who do not subscribe to conventional thinking, or who are different
- need for strong leadership
- belief in simple answers and polemics, i.e. the source of all our problems is the loss of morals
- resistance to creative, dangerous ideas
- tendency to project one's own feelings of inadequacy, rage and fear onto a scapegoated group

To measure these things, Adorno devised a test that asks people to state how much they agree with particular statements. For example:

Q The businessman and the manufacturer are more important to our country than artists and writers.

Q Every person should have complete faith in a supernatural being whose decisions he obeys without question.

The authoritarian personality is servile to people who have superior status, hostile to people who have inferior status and supports conventional values. According to

Exam tip

Be prepared to explain why the authoritarian personality is a dispositional explanation.

Adorno, harsh childrearing practices lead to the authoritarian personality, and people with an authoritarian personality project onto minority groups their unconscious hostility to their parents and their own unacceptable anti-social impulses.

Knowledge check 5

In the Milgram experiment, why may someone with an authoritarian personality be more likely to obey?

Evaluation

Strengths
- It may explain individual differences in obedience to authority.

Limitations
- Harsh childrearing practices cannot explain why whole societies discriminate against minorities, e.g. racism in the USA, anti-Semitism in Germany in the 1930s and 1940s.
- The F-scale is unlikely to be a valid measurement of personality.

Individual differences in obedience or independence

Psychologists propose some predictors of how likely people are to follow orders.

- **Personality.** Adorno suggested that some people have an authoritarian personality, characterised by holding conventional values, being hostile to outgroups, being intolerant to ambiguity and having a submissive attitude to authority. According to Adorno, authoritarian personalities are more likely to obey those in authority.
- **Moral development.** Kohlberg suggested that levels of moral development varied between individuals and that some people reach a level at which their own ethical principles motivate their behaviour. According to Kohlberg, many people operate at a moral level where fear of punishment, or promise of reward, motivate their decisions.

Milgram's findings suggest that people resist authority when:

- the person giving the order is not present or is at a distance (e.g. experimenter instructs teacher by telephone)
- the environment in which the order is given does not have high social prestige (e.g. experiment moved from Yale to a scruffy office)
- there is peer support for disobedience (e.g. other teachers refused to give shocks)
- the person giving the order has no legitimate authority (e.g. experimenter is a member of the public)

Exam tip

Be prepared for an exam question that asks you to suggest two factors that increase independent behaviour.

Summary of factors affecting obedience or independent behaviour

People are more likely to *resist obedience* if they:

- are self-confident and able to act independently
- have a high level of moral development
- have an internal locus of control
- wish to maintain their autonomy and be in control
- have role models who refuse to obey
- are supported by peers who refuse to obey
- are educated as to the dangers of uncritical obedience
- are reminded that they are responsible for the consequences of their actions

Knowledge check 6

Outline two individual differences that may affect independent behaviour.

Explanations of resistance to social influence

Factors that affect social conformity

Situational and personal variables affect the extent to which people conform.

- **Group size.** The bigger the majority, the more influential it is. In a replication of his original study, Asch tested this and found that with only two confederates, the real participants conformed only 13% of the time. With three confederates, the conformity rate rose to 33%, but increasing the number of confederates to more than three had no effect.

- **Gender.** Some research suggests that females conform more than males, because the norm for female behaviour is to be socially orientated (to want to get on with people). However, Eagly and Carli (1981) suggest that experiments that test conformity use tasks that are more familiar to men. The social norms for female behaviour have also changed in the last two decades.

- **Personality.** Some people are more self-confident and have higher self-esteem than others. Asch suggested that students conformed less than non-students. He proposed that having a high IQ might be associated with lower levels of conformity.

- **Locus of control.** People having an **external locus of control** believe that events in their life are outside their control, perhaps being controlled by powerful others, and are more likely to conform or be obedient to those having authority. Those having an **internal locus of control** see themselves as responsible for what happens to them and are more likely to resist pressure to conform and to resist pressure to obey authority.

- **Situational factors.** If we are with others who refuse to obey we are less likely to obey, but if we are with people who obey we are more likely to obey. If we are given an order by someone who cannot see whether we obey or not, we are more likely to disobey (Milgram).

- **Culture.** People raised in collectivist cultures may be more likely to conform than those raised in individualist cultures, because collectivist cultures value interdependence rather than independence. Smith and Bond (1998) found that Belgian students were less likely to conform (by giving wrong answers) than Indian teachers.

> **Exam tip**
>
> An exam question might ask you to suggest two factors that increase or decrease obedience.

> **Knowledge check 7**
>
> Suggest two individual differences that may affect obedience.

Minority influence

Moscovici et al. (1969)

Aim: To find out whether consistency in the minority is an important factor in minority influence.

Procedures: In a laboratory experiment, female student participants were randomly allocated to either a consistent, inconsistent or control condition. There were six participants in each condition, four naïve participants (who formed the majority) and two confederates (the minority). In the control condition there were no confederates. All participants were tested for colour blindness. Participants were asked to name the colour of 36 slides, all of which were blue but which varied in brightness. In the consistent condition the confederates named all 36 slides as green. In the inconsistent condition

→

> **Knowledge check 8**
>
> Which research method did Moscovici use in his study of minority influence?

the confederates named 24 of the slides as green and 12 slides as blue. Minority influence was measured by the percentage of naïve participants' answers that called the blue slides green (i.e. followed the minority influence).

Findings: In the consistent condition 8.42% of the participants' answers were green and 32% gave the incorrect answer at least once. In the inconsistent condition 1.25% of the participants' answers were green. In the control condition only 0.25% of the participants' answers were green. The consistent condition showed the greatest conformity to minority influence.

Conclusions: A minority can influence individuals' behaviour and beliefs and this influence is more likely when the minority is consistent, thus, relating to social change, a consistent minority may influence the majority.

Evaluation

- **Strengths.** The experimental method gives control over variables. Statements can be made about cause and effect. The study can be replicated.
- **Limitations.** The study has low mundane validity; the experimental procedure does not represent a lifelike social situation. People may not be influenced to change their opinions about social situations as easily as they are about the colour of a slide.

The characteristics of influential minorities

Moscovici (1985) suggested five characteristics of the behaviour of influential minorities:

- They are consistent, demonstrating certainty, and they draw attention to their views.
- They enter into discussion and avoid being too dogmatic.
- They take action in support of their principles (e.g. take part in protest marches).
- They make sacrifices to maintain their views.
- They are similar in terms of age, class and gender, to the population they are trying to influence.

The role of social influence processes in social change

The research by Asch, Milgram and Zimbardo can be used to educate people of the danger of 'blind' obedience to authority. Zimbardo and Leippe (1991) propose six steps that can be taken to resist pressure to comply, or pressure to obey an authority figure.

(1) Trust your intuition if and when you feel there is 'something wrong'.

(2) Don't just accept the definition of the situation given to you by a person whose interests may conflict with yours.

(3) Consider the 'worst case' scenario (what could happen if you obey?) and act on that possibility.

Exam tip

In the exam you might be asked to explain how research into minority influence can be applied to understand social change. You could consider whether the characteristics of influential minorities 'fit' a particular pressure group (e.g. Animal Rights, Greenpeace).

Knowledge check 9

Identify two characteristics of an influential minority.

(4) Figure out an 'escape plan' and act on this as soon as possible.

(5) Don't worry about 'what the other person may think of you' — if you are mistaken, you can always apologise when it is safe to do so.

(6) According to Ross (1988), obedience in Milgram would have been reduced had there been an 'exit button' visible and in easy reach of the participants, who could have pressed it when they wanted to stop.

Think about this 'exit button' idea, and mentally rehearse it as it applies to situations in your life.

Exam tip

In the exam you could be asked to describe and evaluate two studies of social influence.

Social influence: glossary of terms

agentic state: when a person acts as the agent (or tool) of a person having legitimate authority and holds the authority figure responsible for their actions, he or she is in an 'agentic state'.

compliance: this occurs when a person conforms to the majority opinion in public but in private does not agree. If group pressure is removed, the conformity will cease. Compliance is thought to occur because an individual wishes to be accepted by the majority group.

deindividuation: the loss of a person's sense of individuality. For instance, in the Zimbardo experiment the prisoners and guards lost the sense of 'who they were' in their everyday lives.

identification: conforming to the behaviour expected by the majority, such as obeying school rules about uniform, but without enthusiasm. Identification is thought to occur because an individual wishes to belong to a group.

informational social influence: this occurs when a question asked does not have an obviously correct answer. When this happens, people look to others for information and may agree with the majority view.

internalisation: this occurs when an individual conforms because he or she believes that a group norm for behaviour or a group attitude is 'right'. If group pressure is removed, this conformity will continue.

learned helplessness: the feeling that nothing that one does will change the situation one is in, as in the Zimbardo experiment when the unpredictable decisions of the guards led the prisoners to become passive and depressed.

legitimate authority: when a person giving an order (e.g. a policeman or headteacher) is perceived as having the 'right' to tell others how to behave, they have legitimate authority.

majority influence (conformity): the process that takes place when the views of the dominant group affect an individual's attitudes or behaviour. This may be because of **normative social influence** (the effect of social norms), but can also occur because of **informational social influence** (when the minority yield to group pressure because they think that the majority has more knowledge or information).

minority influence: the process that takes place when a consistent minority changes the attitudes and/or behaviour of an individual. Social psychologists propose that it is the consistency of the minority that is important, since it demonstrates a firm, alternative view to that of the majority. Minority influence leads to a change in attitudes and involves the process of conversion.

normative social influence: this occurs when an individual agrees with the opinions of a group of people because he or she wishes to be accepted by them. The influenced individual may not change his or her private belief.

obedience: a change in behaviour so that people do what a person having authority tells them to do.

slippery slope: the course a person takes when he or she follows a small reasonable order, and then feels obliged to continue to obey when the orders gradually become unreasonable.

social influence: the way that a person or a group of people affect the attitudes and behaviour of another individual.

Knowledge summary

You should be able to:
- describe conformity (majority influence) and explain why people conform
- differentiate between informational social influence and normative social influence
- identify and describe and differentiate between types of conformity and explain the difference between internalisation and compliance
- describe and evaluate research into obedience to authority, including Milgram's work
- identify and explain situational and dispositional reasons why people obey

- explain independent behaviour, including locus of control
- explain why people resist pressures to conform and resist pressures to obey authority
- discuss, using evidence, how social influence research helps us to understand social change
- describe and evaluate research into minority influence and identify the characteristics of influential minorities
- discuss how majority and minority influence can affect social change

■Memory

This topic is examined on AS Paper 1 and on A-level Paper 1.

Short-term memory and long-term memory

Psychologists distinguish between **short-term memory** (STM) and **long-term memory** (LTM). STM cannot hold much information and has limited capacity, whereas LTM can hold an apparently unlimited amount of information and has a vast capacity. George Miller theorised that the capacity of STM is approximately 'seven plus or minus two' pieces of information, but that this capacity can be extended by chunking, or combining, small pieces of information.

The table below shows some of the ways in which STM and LTM are different.

Comparison	Short-term memory (STM)	Long-term memory (LTM)
Capacity	Limited (7 ± 2 chunks)	Potentially unlimited
Duration	Short (seconds only)	Possibly lifelong
Encoding	Acoustic (sound)	Semantic (meaning)

Comparison of short- and long-term memory

A study of encoding in STM and LTM (Baddeley 1966)

Aims: To show that STM is largely based on acoustic code; to find out whether LTM is also acoustically encoded, and to find out whether STM or LTM is semantically encoded.

Procedures: Participants were given four sets of words to recall: (1) acoustically similar (e.g. cap, can, map); (2) acoustically dissimilar (e.g. pit, cow, pen); (3) semantically similar (e.g. big, huge, large); (4) semantically dissimilar (e.g. good, hot, safe). One group was asked to recall words immediately (from STM) and a second group was asked to recall words after a delay of 20 minutes (from LTM).

Findings: The immediate recall (STM) group remembered fewer acoustically similar than acoustically dissimilar words. The delayed recall (LTM) group showed no significant difference when remembering acoustically encoded words but differences in semantically encoded words.

Conclusions: Findings suggest acoustic encoding in STM but semantic encoding in LTM.

Criticisms: Control in laboratory experiments facilitates the identification of cause-and-effect relationships, thus the findings have high internal validity. However, laboratory experiments into memory only involve memory of facts rather than memory of experiences, thus because the findings apply only to limited aspects of memory, they have low external validity.

Exam tip

Rosy read out three random letters to Paul and asked him to repeat these, then four, five, six, seven, eight letters, and so on. When she read out ten letters, Paul could not remember them all. In an exam you could be asked to explain what Rosy was measuring.

A study of capacity in STM (Jacobs 1987)

Aim: To research the capacity of STM.

Procedures: Participants were presented with strings of letters or digits and were asked to repeat them back in the same order. The length of the string was increased, from three to four, five, six etc., until the participant was unable to repeat the sequence accurately.

Findings: On average, participants recalled nine digits and seven letters. The average recall increased with age.

Conclusions: STM has a limited storage capacity of between five and nine items, but learned memory techniques (e.g. chunking) may increase capacity as people get older.

Criticisms: The research is artificial. In real-life settings people do not usually need to remember strings of meaningless numbers or letters, and the research therefore has low ecological validity. If the information to be remembered has more meaning, it might be remembered better.

Knowledge check 10

Outline the capacity of memory in STM.

A study of duration in LTM (Bahrick et al. 1975)

Aim: To study very long-term memories in a real-life setting.

Procedures: There were three tasks: (1) In a free recall test, 392 people were asked to list the names of their ex-classmates. (2) In a photo recognition task, participants were shown photographs of their ex-classmates and asked if they could remember the names. (3) In a name recognition task, participants were given names of their ex-classmates and asked to find the matching photographs.

Findings: Within 15 years of leaving school, participants could recognise 90% of the faces and names. Within 48 years of leaving school, participants could recognise 75% of the faces and names. Free recall memory had declined more than photo and name recognition memory.

Conclusions: The study shows evidence of very long-term memories in a real-life setting. Since recognition was more accurate than free recall, there may be information stored in memory that can be accessed only when we are given an appropriate cue.

Criticisms: This study was undertaken in a real-life setting and the memories were meaningful to the participants, so it has high ecological validity. It also has application in real life: for example, carers could show elderly people photographs of their friends and colleagues in the Second World War in order to engage them in conversation.

Exam tip

In the exam you could be asked to describe how psychologists investigate the duration of short-term memory. In your answer, include details of what the participants are asked to do and how duration of memory is measured.

Knowledge check 11

Outline two differences between STM and LTM.

The multi-store model of memory (Atkinson and Shiffrin 1968)

Models, or theories, of memory aim to explain how information is transferred from STM to LTM, and why sometimes it is not.

In their **multi-store model of memory**, Atkinson and Shiffrin suggest that memory comprises three separate stores: the sensory memory store, the STM and the LTM. Each store has a specific function, as shown in Figure 1.

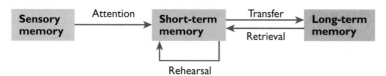

Figure 1 Multi-store model

In the multi-store model, information is rehearsed in STM and, if rehearsed enough, is transferred to LTM.

There are three stages of information processing in the multi-store model of memory:

Stage 1: sensory information is perceived (seen, heard etc.)

Stage 2: the sensory information is transferred to STM, where it is maintained by rehearsal (if it is not lost or replaced by new, incoming information).

Stage 3: the information is transferred to LTM.

Exam tip

Make sure you can draw and label a diagram of the multi-store model of memory.

Research evidence (Glanzer and Cunitz 1966)

Participants were asked to recall word lists. When words were recalled immediately, early and later words were more likely to be recalled (primacy and recency effect) due to STM and LTM effects.

Primacy effect occurs because the first words are likely to have been transferred to LTM. **Recency effect** occurs because the last words in the list are still in STM. If there was a delay of 10 seconds or more before recall, there was only a primacy effect — only LTM was affected. This demonstrates a difference between STM and LTM.

Evaluation

- A strength of the multi-store model is that it is simple and can be tested. Research evidence supports the idea that STM and LTM are qualitatively different types of memory. Moreover, we have all, from time to time, 'rehearsed' information and it seems to make sense that rehearsed information is more likely to be remembered.
- However, a weakness is that, in real life, memories are created in contexts rather different from laboratory-based 'free recall' experiments, so perhaps this model does not explain fully the complexities of human memory. In addition, the model suggests that memory is a passive process, whereas theories of reconstructive memory suggest that memory is an active process.

Knowledge check 12

Explain why the primacy and recency effects provide evidence for the multi-store model of memory.

Types of long-term memory

Psychologists theorise that there are three different types of long-term memory — **episodic, semantic and procedural.**

Episodic memory

Episodic memory is the memory of autobiographical events (e.g. times, places, associated emotions, and other contextual who, what, when, where, why knowledge) that can be explicitly stated. It is the collection of past personal experiences that occurred at a particular time and place. For example, if you remember your year 11 prom, or your first driving lesson, this is an episodic memory. Using episodic memory you become a time-machine as you travel back in time to remember past events. Recollection is one of the main components of episodic memory and during recollection we retrieve contextual information pertaining to a specific event or experience.

Semantic memory

Semantic memory refers to the memory of meaning and understanding and semantic and episodic memory make up the category called **declarative memory (explicit memory)**. With the use of our semantic memory we can give meaning to otherwise meaningless words and sentences. Semantic memory includes generalised knowledge that does not involve memory of a specific event. For instance, semantic memory contains information about what a horse is, whereas episodic memory might contain a specific memory of riding a specific horse.

Procedural memory

Procedural memory is a part of the long-term memory that is responsible for knowing how to do things (motor skills). Procedural memory stores information on how to perform certain procedures, such as walking, talking, typing, playing the piano, riding a bike. Procedural memories are implicit and do not involve conscious thought. Procedural memory is also important in language development, as it allows a person to talk without having to give much thought to proper grammar and syntax.

The working memory model (Baddeley and Hitch 1974)

The Baddeley and Hitch model of working memory is more complex than the multi-store model, but it focuses solely on STM or, as Baddeley and Hitch call it, **working memory**. They propose a multi-store model of STM. In their model, STM is an active processor in which the central executive 'attends to and works on' either speech-based information passed to it from the articulatory–phonological loop or visually coded information passed to it by the visual system. The three components of this model are as follows:

- The **central executive** processes information from all sensory routes; this process is 'attention-like', having limited capacity.
- The **articulatory–phonological loop** processes speech-based information. The phonological store focuses on speech perception (incoming speech) and the articulatory process focuses on speech production.
- The **visuospatial working area** (also known as the 'visuospatial sketchpad' or 'scratchpad') is where spatial and visual information is processed.

Exam tip

Make sure you can explain the difference between these three types of long-term memory.

Knowledge check 13

Which of these three types of long-term memory do not involve conscious thought?

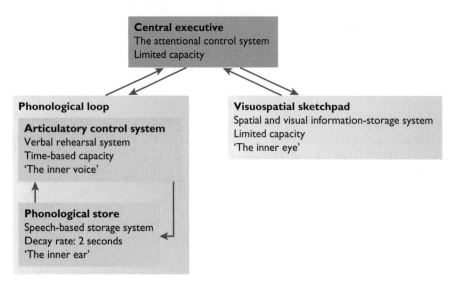

Figure 2 The working memory model

The working memory model can be tested by the **interference task** technique. This technique is based on the assumption that the articulatory–phonological loop and the visuospatial scratchpad both have limited capacity to process information, so when participants are asked to perform two tasks, using the same system at the same time, their performance is affected. For instance, repeating 'the' silently while reading is difficult because both of these tasks use the articulatory–phonological loop, which has limited capacity; it cannot cope with both tasks, so the performance of one or the other will be affected.

> **Exam tip**
>
> In the exam you may need to describe the different functions of the central executive, the articulatory–phonological loop and the visuospatial working area.

Evaluation

Strengths
- It suggests that rehearsal is an optional process, which is more realistic than the multi-store model, especially since we do not rehearse everything that we remember.
- The model can explain how we can successfully do two tasks at the same time if the tasks involve different stores, but why we have trouble performing two tasks at the same time if the tasks involve the same store.

Weaknesses
- Least is known about the precise function of the most important component, the central executive, and the suggestion that there may be a single central executive may be inaccurate.

> **Exam tip**
>
> Make sure you can describe the three components of the working memory model.

You should be able to refer to the working memory model to explain why a brain scan shows that, when someone is performing a verbal task, a different part of the brain is active than when performing a visual task.

Explain how the interference task technique can be used to find evidence to support the working memory model.

Explanations for forgetting

Why do we forget? First, possibly, because the memory has disappeared, and is no longer available. Second, possibly the memory is still stored but, for some reason, it cannot be retrieved. The first answer is more likely to be applied to forgetting in short-term memory, the second to forgetting in long-term memory.

Interference theory

Memory can be disrupted or interfered with by what we have previously learned or by what we learn in the future. This theory suggests that information in long-term memory may become confused or combined with other information during encoding, thus distorting or disrupting memories.

Interference theory states that forgetting occurs because memories interfere with one another. There are two ways in which interference can cause forgetting:

- **Proactive interference** occurs when you cannot learn a new task because what you already know interferes with what you are currently learning — where old memories disrupt new memories.
- **Retroactive interference** occurs when you forget a previously learned task due to the learning of a new task — later learning interferes with earlier learning or new memories disrupt old memories.

Proactive and retroactive interference are thought to be more likely to occur when the memories are similar, for example, confusing old and new telephone numbers.

A study of retroactive interference (Postman 1960)

Aim: To investigate how retroactive interference affects learning. In other words, to investigate whether information you have recently received interferes with the ability to recall something you learned earlier.

Procedure: In a laboratory experiment participants were split into two groups. Both groups had to remember a list of paired words (e.g. cat – tree, jelly – moss, book – tractor). The experimental group also had to learn another list of words where the second paired word was different (e.g. cat – glass, jelly – time, book – revolver). The control group was not given the second list. All participants were asked to recall the words on the first list.

Findings: The recall of the control group was more accurate than that of the experimental group.

Conclusion: This suggests that learning items in the second list interfered with participants' ability to recall the list. This is an example of retroactive interference.

Criticism: Although supported by experimental evidence, there are a number of problems with interference theory as an explanation of forgetting:

- Interference theory does not help us to understand the cognitive processes involved in forgetting.
- Most research into the role of interference in forgetting has been carried out in a laboratory using lists of words — a situation which is likely to occur fairly infrequently in everyday life (i.e. low ecological validity).
- Baddeley (1990) states that the laboratory tasks given to participants are too similar to each other and that in everyday life these kinds of events are more spaced out. There is no doubt that interference plays a role in forgetting, but how much forgetting can be explained by interference remains unclear.

Forgetting due to retrieval failure

Retrieval failure is where the information is in long-term memory, but cannot be accessed (remembered) because the retrieval cues are not present. A retrieval cue is a hint or clue that can help retrieval.

When we store a new memory we also store information about the situation. These are known as **retrieval cues**. When we come to the same situation again, these retrieval cues can trigger the memory of the situation. Retrieval cues can be:

- **external/context** — cues in the environment, e.g. smell, place
- **internal/state** — cues inside us, e.g. physical, emotional, mood

Psychologists suggest that information is more likely to be retrieved from long-term memory if appropriate retrieval cues are present. Tulving (1974) argued that information would be more easily retrieved if the cues present when the information was encoded were also present when the memory is retrieved. Tulving suggested that information about the physical surroundings (external context) and about the physical or psychological state of the person (internal context) is stored at the same time as memory is formed. Therefore, reinstating the state or context makes recall easier, but retrieval failure occurs when appropriate cues are not present.

Context (external) cues

Retrieval cues may be based on context, the setting or situation in which information is encoded and retrieved. Examples include a particular room, or a certain group of people or the way information is presented. Evidence indicates that retrieval is more likely when the context at encoding matches the context at retrieval.

A number of experiments have indicated the importance of context-based cues for retrieval. An experiment conducted by Tulving and Pearlstone (1966) asked participants to learn lists of words belonging to different categories, for example names of animals, clothing and sports.

Participants were then asked to recall the words. Those who were given the category names recalled substantially more words than those who were not. The categories

Knowledge check 15

Simeon had two language (vocabulary) tests. In the morning he revised his French vocabulary and after lunch he revised his Spanish vocabulary. In the test he did poorly in his French but better in his Spanish. Explain how retroactive interference may have affected his French test.

provided a context, and naming the categories provided retrieval cues. Tulving and Pearlstone argued that **cue-dependent forgetting** explains the difference between the two groups of participants. Those who recalled fewer words lacked appropriate retrieval cues.

An experiment conducted by Baddeley (1975) indicates the importance of setting for retrieval. Baddeley asked deep-sea divers to memorise a list of words. One group did this on the beach and the other group underwater. When they were asked to remember the words half of the beach learners remained on the beach, the rest had to recall underwater. Half of the underwater group remained there and the others had to recall on the beach.

The results show that those who had recalled in the same environment (i.e. context) in which they had learned recalled 40% more words than those recalling in a different environment. This suggests that the retrieval of information is improved if it occurs in the context in which it was learned.

Knowledge check 16

Can you explain what is meant by a 'retrieval cue' and explain the difference between **external (context)** retrieval cues and **internal (state)** retrieval cues?

> **Exam tip**
>
> In a classroom, 20 students were given a list of 30 flower names to memorise and then given 1 minute to write down all the ones they could remember: 10 students stayed in the same classroom for the memory test but 10 were taken to a different room. Based on what you have learned about forgetting, you should be able to explain why the students who stayed in the same room remembered more of the flower names.

The accuracy of eyewitness testimony

Research into eyewitness testimony (Loftus and Palmer 1974)

Loftus and Palmer conducted research into the accuracy of **eyewitness testimony** (EWT). In experiment 1 they investigated the effect of **leading questions** on eyewitness accounts, and in experiment 2 they investigated the effects that leading questions have on later memory of what happened. The leading question they asked was based on 'How fast were the cars going when they smashed into each other?' but the verb 'smashed' was varied to lead participants to perceive different speeds for the vehicles.

Experiment 1

Forty-five student participants viewed a short video of a car accident. The participants were divided into five groups of nine students. After watching the video, each group was given a questionnaire that included the leading question. However, a slightly different version of the critical question was given to each group, in that the verb varied between 'smashed', 'collided', 'bumped', 'hit' and 'contacted'. As shown in the bar chart, the leading question affected the participants' perception of speed. The conclusion was that the way questions are worded may affect perception and recall.

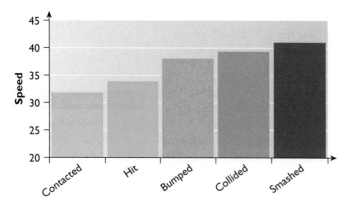

Figure 3 Experiment 1: estimated speed for verb used

Experiment 2

One hundred and fifty student participants (three groups of 50) viewed a short video of a car accident. Afterwards they were given a questionnaire. Again, the critical leading question was based on 'How fast were the cars going when they smashed into each other?' However, group 1 was asked the critical question containing the word 'hit', group 2 was asked it with the word 'smashed' and group 3 (the control group) was not asked the leading question.

A week later, the participants were asked to return and answer more questions, including 'Did you see any broken glass?' (there was no broken glass in the film clip). The findings are shown in the bar chart. Those participants who thought the car was travelling faster (the 'smashed' group) were more likely to report seeing broken glass. This suggests that their memory of a car travelling faster led them to 'invent' a memory in line with this expectation.

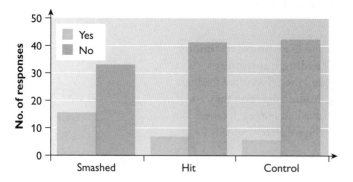

Figure 4 Experiment 2: response to 'Did you see any broken glass?'

The findings from these two experiments suggest that leading questions do have an effect on what eyewitnesses think they have seen.

Criticism: There is some evidence from real-life studies that recall is not affected by leading questions — perhaps because emotional arousal makes the original image stronger. However, the high levels of control in the laboratory experiment meant that it was possible to show clearly that EWT could be affected by the way questions were asked. The results have a useful application in real life — when the testimony of an eyewitness could lead to a person being convicted of a crime.

Exam tip

You should be able to explain what the findings of experiment 1 suggest in terms of EWT.

Knowledge check 17

Can you describe how the false memory was created in experiment 2?

Exam tip

Make sure you can explain why the findings of the second experiment have increased validity when suggesting that leading questions can change the memory of an event.

Eyewitness memory of a crime (Yuille and Cutshall 1986)

Aim: To examine eyewitness accounts of a real event.

Sample: 21 witnesses to a gun-shooting crime were interviewed by police. Four to five months after the incident, 20 witnesses were contacted and 13 agreed to be re-interviewed; 10 were male and 3 female and their ages ranged from 15 to 32.

Method: Case study of a real event (shooting). The initial police interviews were made available to the researchers and included a verbatim account of the event in the witness's words and their responses to a series of questions designed to clarify aspects of the event.

Research interviews were conducted 4–5 months after the event at a time and place chosen by the witness. Interviews were between 45 and 90 minutes long and followed the same procedures as the police interview: an account in the witness's own words followed by questions to clarify earlier points and solicit specific details. The questions included two misleading ones. One misleading question asked about a broken headlight: 6 of the witnesses were asked if they had seen 'the busted headlight' and the remainder were asked if they had seen 'a busted headlight' (there was no broken headlight). Another similar question was asked about a differently coloured panel on the car. These questions were chosen because, although the car was in full view of all the witnesses, the car did not play a major part in the event.

Scoring: The event was reconstructed from police evidence (photographs, confiscated weapons, witness descriptions etc.) and reports of other professionals attending the scene (ambulance men etc). Each detail recalled was awarded 1 point.

Results: The research interview elicited considerably more detail than the police interview:
- Police interviews: number of details recalled   649.5
- Research interviews: number of details recalled 1,056.5

Misleading questions had no effect.

Conclusion: This is a very different finding from most of the laboratory research conducted into EWT. There was a small amount of information reported that never happened (2.93% of action details reported to police, 3.23% in research interviews), but this is lower than is often reported by laboratory research.

> **Knowledge check 18**
>
> Outline two differences between the research by Loftus and Palmer and the Yuille and Cutshall research.

Factors that may influence eyewitness memory

- **Estimator and system variables.** These two main reasons for witness error were proposed by Wells (1978). **Estimator variables** are factors to do with the witness. They might include levels of stress and whether or not the criminal was carrying a weapon. **System variables** are factors where the justice system has some control, such as preventing the use of leading questions (e.g. Loftus and Palmer 1974).
- **Duration of event and time of day.** The longer we watch, the more likely we are to remember details. Witnesses also remember more when they see something during the day or at night, but twilight is not very good. It seems that people make more effort when it is dark because they know that viewing conditions are poor.

- **Violence distraction.** People have a better memory for non-violent events. Clifford and Scott (1978) showed their participants two short films, one violent and one not, and participants remembered more about the non-violent film.
- **The amount of time between an event and recall.** This will influence memory — the longer the time, the worse the recall. This is known as **trace-dependent forgetting**. Over time, the memory trace will disappear because when memory circuits are not activated for long periods, the connections between them may weaken to the point where the circuit is broken and the information is lost.
- **Anxiety (stress).** Highly emotional events may be either more memorable or less memorable than everyday events. **Flashbulb memories** can be described as memories of emotional events that last for a lifetime. Christianson and Hubinette (1993) found that emotional involvement does increase the accuracy of memory. They interviewed 110 people who had witnessed a bank robbery. Witnesses who had been personally threatened during the crime, and who were more emotionally involved, had more accurate memories than the witnesses who said they were not very involved. However, Freud suggested that **repression** is the way we protect our ego (conscious mind) from unpleasant memories, and that unhappy or traumatic memories are more likely to be forgotten because we are unconsciously motivated to forget events that make us uncomfortable.
- **Age of a witness.** Some research suggests that age affects how well people remember events. Cohen and Faulkner (1989) showed two groups of participants a film of a kidnapping. The average age of one group of participants was 70. The average age of the second group of participants was 35. Both groups were asked leading questions when they were questioned about the film. The older participants were significantly more likely to be misled by the leading questions.

> **Exam tip**
>
> You may find it helpful to make a chart identifying the factors that influence eyewitness memory and why these factors affect memory.

Improving the accuracy of eyewitness testimony

The cognitive interview (Geiselman 1985)

The **cognitive interview** is a procedure used by the police to help eyewitnesses recall information more accurately. During the interview the witness is encouraged to:

- report every detail, no matter how seemingly trivial
- recreate the context of the event
- recall the event in different orders (in reverse, partially etc.)
- recall the event from other perspectives (imagining what someone in a different place may have seen)

While the interview is progressing, the police take care to:

- reduce the anxiety felt by witnesses
- minimise any distractions
- allow the witness to take his or her time
- avoid interruptions and leading questions

This type of interview has been found to achieve up to 35% improvement in the accuracy of recall, especially if the interview takes place shortly after the event.

Research evidence: the cognitive interview (Fisher et al. 1989)

Aim: To test the validity of the cognitive interview technique.

Procedures: 16 experienced police officers from Florida USA interviewed 47 witnesses or victims of shoplifting or mugging twice. Between the two interviews, 7 officers were trained to use the cognitive interview technique; the other 9 officers formed the control group. The independent variable was the type of interview, cognitive or standard, while the dependent variable was the number of accurately recorded facts elicited in the interview. The difference in the number of facts in the second interview was measured and two comparisons were made: (1) did the second interview gain more facts than the first interview? (2) did the cognitive interview gain more facts than the standard interview?

Findings: The cognitive interview gained 47% more facts than were gained in the first standard interview. There was no gain in facts in the second standard interview by the control group.

Conclusion: The cognitive interview is a useful technique for improving EWT.

Criticism: These were real officers and real witnesses, leading to high external validity. However, the control group officers were aware that they had not received training and this may have affected their motivation levels.

Memory: glossary of terms

capacity: a measure of how much information can be stored in STM and LTM. Capacity of STM is thought to be 7 ± 2 chunks of information. LTM is thought to have unlimited capacity for many types of information.

cognitive interview: a procedure used by the police to help eyewitnesses recall information more accurately. During the interview the witness is encouraged to relax and recall everything they can remember, no matter how trivial the information appears. During recall the police do not ask questions or interrupt the witness.

duration: a measure of how long information is held in memory. In STM the duration of information, if not rehearsed, is very short — less than 30 seconds. In LTM the duration of information may be a lifetime.

encoding: the form in which information is stored in memory. In STM information is thought to be stored in acoustic code (by sound). In LTM information is thought to be stored in semantic code (by meaning).

eyewitness testimony (EWT): descriptions of events given by people who were present at the time (e.g. in criminal trials). Eyewitness descriptions may include descriptions of people, places, sequences of events and other information.

flashbulb memory: an accurate and long-lasting memory of the details of the context of an event created at a time of intense emotion — as if a flash photograph has been taken where every detail is printed in memory.

Exam tip

Make sure you can explain how the cognitive interview may increase the number of retrieval cues and thus help witnesses recall information.

Knowledge check 19

Outline how a cognitive interview is used to investigate memory of an event, including *at least one* example of what a participant would be asked to do.

leading question: a question that suggests a certain kind of answer. For example, 'Was the burglar's hat black or brown?' suggests that the burglar was wearing a hat.

levels of processing: the suggestion that the duration of a memory is dependent on the way that information is processed, and that if information is processed deeply (e.g. organised or elaborated in some way), it will be remembered for longer.

long-term memory (LTM): relatively permanent memory that has unlimited capacity and duration.

memory: the process by which we retain information, including encoding, storage and retrieval of experiences.

multi-store model of memory: the model of memory which proposes that information enters our mind through sensory perception, and is then passed to a short-term store (STM) where it is held for a brief duration unless rehearsed. Rehearsal leads to transfer to a long-term store (LTM).

proactive interference: this occurs when you cannot learn a new task because what you already know interferes with what you are currently learning — where old memories disrupt new memories.

reconstructive memory: an explanation of how we store and remember long-term memories in terms of social and cultural processes, which explains why both the creation of a memory and later recall may be distorted by schemas and stereotypes.

repression: a method of keeping anxiety-provoking information out of conscious awareness — called 'motivated forgetting'. Freud proposed that repression is an ego-defence mechanism and that repressed information may surface in dreams or in Freudian slips.

retroactive interference: this occurs when you forget a previously learned task due to the learning of a new task — in other words, later learning interferes with earlier learning or new memories disrupt old memories.

short-term memory (STM): a temporary store for information which is limited in capacity (7 ± 2 chunks of information) and duration (probably less than 30 seconds). Information in STM is thought to be stored acoustically (by sounds) rather than semantically (by meaning).

working memory model: a model of STM which suggests that one area of memory processes the information we are currently working on. This information is processed by a phonological loop (acoustic data) and/or by a visuospatial scratchpad (visual data). Both the phonological loop and the visuospatial scratchpad are organised by a central executive.

Knowledge summary

You should be able to:
- describe and evaluate the multi-store model of memory
- explain the concepts of memory encoding, capacity and duration
- describe and evaluate the working memory model
- differentiate between the multi-store model of memory and the working memory model
- explain how proactive interference and retroactive interference may lead to forgetting
- suggest how retrieval cues help us remember information

- define what is meant by eyewitness memory
- describe and evaluate research into eyewitness memory
- identify factors affecting the accuracy of EWT
- explain how misleading information and anxiety can affect EWT
- describe psychological research into improving accuracy of EWT
- describe the procedures involved in a cognitive interview and explain why the cognitive interview should increase the accuracy of witness recall

■Attachment

This topic is examined on AS Paper 1 and on A-level Paper 1.

Developmental psychologists study the changes that occur as people grow from childhood, through adolescence, and into adulthood. **Attachments**, which are strong emotional bonds that form as a result of interaction between two people, occur throughout our life span. Schaffer (1993) defines attachment as 'a close emotional relationship between two persons characterised by mutual affection and a desire to maintain closeness'. Psychologists have proposed two main theories to explain attachment:

- Learning/behaviourist theory of attachment. This suggests that attachment is learned behaviour. The basis for the learning of attachments is the provision of food. An infant will initially form an attachment to whoever feeds it and learns to associate the feeder (usually the mother) with the comfort of being fed and, through the process of classical conditioning, learns to find contact with the mother comforting.
- Evolutionary theory of attachment. This suggests that infants come into the world biologically pre-programmed to form attachments with others, because this will help them to survive. The infant produces innate 'social releaser' behaviours such as crying and smiling that stimulate innate caregiving responses from adults.

Caregiver–infant interaction

Interaction between caregiver and infant helps to develop and maintain attachment. Interactions include reciprocity, imitation, interactional synchrony and the use of modified language:

- **Interactional synchrony and reciprocity.** Condon and Sander (1974) analysed the movements of babies while adults were speaking to them. They found that the babies 'moved in time' with the conversation and appeared to 'take turns'. They described this as reciprocal behaviour. Reciprocal behaviour is behaviour that is produced as a response to the behaviour of another person or behaviour that is produced to elicit a response from another person.
- **Imitation.** Melzoff and Moore (1977) found that 2–3-week-old babies spontaneously imitated adult facial expressions and movements.
- **Modified language.** Caregivers modify their language and use 'motherese' when they speak to young babies. Motherese is a slow, high-pitched, repetitive way of speaking in short, simple sentences and varying tone. The use of motherese may aid communication and may contribute to effective turn-taking and aid attachment.

Evaluation

- Studies with animals (Harlow's monkeys) suggest that infant–caregiver interaction is important for the development of attachment.
- Even if babies do imitate facial expressions this imitation may not be intentional communication.
- Adults use motherese with all babies and with young children and there is no direct evidence that the use of motherese influences attachment.

Research into interactional synchrony during the infant's first year (Isabella et al. 1989)

Aim: To test the hypothesis that synchronous infant–mother interaction is associated with secure attachment while non-synchronous infant–mother interaction is associated with insecure attachment.

Method: The study observed infants at 1, 3 and 9 months old while interacting with their caregiver (mother). Thirty infant–mother pairs were studied.

Findings: Findings from 30 pairs (10 secure, 10 avoidant, 10 resistant) supported the hypothesis at 1 and 3 months, with synchronous interaction observed at significantly frequent rates for securely attached infants. Mother–infant pairs who were developing secure attachments were observed to interact in a well-timed, reciprocal, and mutually rewarding manner, but those developing insecure relationships were characterised by interactions in which mothers were minimally involved or unresponsive to infant signals. The study also identified consistent aspects of interaction (e.g. responsiveness) that differentiated mothers of secure, avoidant, and resistant babies.

Criticism: The study ignores individual differences such as the temperament of the infants. The study is correlational and as such cannot say that the style of mother–infant interaction causes differences in attachment.

> **Exam tip**
> Make sure you can explain how caregiver–infant interaction may influence the development of attachment.

> **Knowledge check 20**
> Define interactional synchrony.

Stages of attachment

Rudolph Schaffer and Peggy Emerson (1964) studied 60 babies at monthly intervals for the first 18 months of life (a longitudinal study).

The children were all studied in their own home and a regular pattern was identified in the development of attachment. The babies were visited monthly for approximately 1 year, their interactions with their caregivers were observed, and caregivers were interviewed.

The study discovered that a baby's attachments develop in the following sequence:

- **Up to 3 months of age** — indiscriminate attachments. The newborn is predisposed to attach to any human. Most babies respond equally to any caregiver.
- **After 4 months** — preference for certain people. Infants learn to distinguish primary and secondary caregivers but accept care from anyone.
- **After 7 months** — special preference for a single attachment figure. The baby looks to particular people for security, comfort and protection. It shows fear of strangers (stranger fear) and unhappiness when separated from a special person (separation anxiety). Some babies show stranger fear and separation anxiety much more frequently and intensely than others, but nevertheless they are seen as evidence that the baby has formed an attachment. This has usually developed by 1 year of age.
- **After 9 months** — multiple attachments. The baby becomes increasingly independent and forms several attachments.

The results of the study indicated that attachments were most likely to form with those who responded accurately to the baby's signals, not the person the baby spent most time with. Schaffer and Emerson called this sensitive responsiveness.

Many of the babies had several attachments by 10 months old, including attachments to mothers, fathers, grandparents, siblings and neighbours. The mother was the main attachment figure for about half of the children at 18 months old and the father for most of the others. The most important fact in forming attachments is not who feeds and changes the child but who plays and communicates with him or her.

Knowledge check 21

Outline the stages of attachment and identify the age at which the child develops multiple attachments.

Animal studies of attachment

Research evidence (Harlow's monkeys 1958)

Aim: To study the mechanisms by which newborn rhesus monkeys bond to their mothers. These infants are highly dependent on their mothers for nutrition, protection, comfort and socialisation but Harlow wanted to find the underlying basis for the attachment.

The behavioural theory of attachment suggests that an infant would form an attachment with a carer who provides food. The evolutionary theory suggests that infants have an innate (biological) need to touch and cling to something for emotional comfort.

Procedures: Harlow did a number of studies on attachment in rhesus monkeys during the 1950s and 1960s:

(1) Infant monkeys reared in isolation — some died, others were frightened and behaved in an abnormal manner. They could not interact with other monkeys even when they were older.

(2) Infant monkeys reared with surrogate mothers — eight monkeys were separated from their mothers immediately after birth and placed in cages with access to two surrogate mothers, one made of wire and one covered in soft terry towelling cloth. Four of the monkeys could get milk from the wire mother and four from the cloth mother. The animals were studied for 165 days.

Findings: Both groups of monkeys spent more time with the cloth mother (even if she had no milk). The infant would only go to the wire mother when hungry. Once fed it would return to the cloth mother for most of the day. If a frightening object was placed in the cage the infant took refuge with the cloth mother. The cloth mother was more effective in decreasing the youngsters' fear. The infant would explore more when the cloth mother was present. This supports the evolutionary theory of attachment, in that it is the sensitive response and security of the caregiver that is important rather than the provision of food.

Conclusion: Harlow concluded that for monkeys to develop normally they must have some interaction with an object to which they can cling during the first months of life (critical period). Clinging is a natural response and in times of stress the monkey runs to the object to which it normally clings. However, Harlow also concluded that the young monkeys suffered from social deprivation rather than maternal deprivation because when he brought other infant monkeys up on their own but with 20 minutes a day in a playroom with three other monkeys he found they grew up to be emotionally and socially normal.

Evaluation

- The experiments have been seen as unnecessarily cruel (unethical) and of limited value in attempting to understand the effects of deprivation on human infants. The monkeys in this study suffered from emotional harm from being reared in isolation.
- However, Harlow's experiment does provide a valuable insight into the development of attachment and social behaviour. It could be argued that the benefits of the research outweigh the costs (suffering of the animals). For example, the research influenced Bowlby, the most important psychologist in attachment theory. It can also be seen as a vital step in convincing people about the importance of emotional care in hospitals, children's homes and day care.

Exam tip

Make sure you can explain what Harlow concluded about whether attachment is based on nature or nurture and why.

Knowledge check 22

Describe the difference between the two surrogate mothers.

Lorenz's imprinting theory

Lorenz (1935) took a large clutch of goose eggs which were ready to hatch and placed half of the eggs under a goose mother, and the other eggs beside himself until the geese hatched. When the geese hatched Lorenz imitated a mother goose quacking and the young birds regarded him as their mother and followed him accordingly. The other group followed the mother goose. Lorenz put all the goslings together under an upturned box and allowed them to mix. When the box was removed the two groups separated to go to their respective 'mothers' — half to the goose, and half to Lorenz.

Lorenz found that geese follow the first moving object they see during a 12–17-hour critical period after hatching. This process is known as **imprinting**, and suggests that attachment is innate and programmed genetically. Imprinting occurs without any feeding taking place and has consequences both for short-term survival and in the longer term for forming internal templates for later relationships. If no attachment has developed within 32 hours it is unlikely any attachment will ever develop.

There seems to be a critical period during which imprinting can occur. Hess (1958) showed that although the imprinting process could occur as early as 1 hour after hatching, the strongest responses occurred between 12 and 17 hours after hatching, and that after 32 hours the response was unlikely to occur at all. Lorenz and Hess believe that once imprinting has occurred it cannot be reversed, nor can a gosling imprint on anything else.

The function of imprinting is probably to enable the animal to recognise close kin. In the natural environment behavioural imprinting results in the formation of a strong bond between offspring and parent. The parent must recognise the offspring in order not to waste time and energy caring for the young of others. The offspring must recognise its parent because it might be attacked and even killed by other adults of the same species that do not recognise it as their own. Imprinting ensures that a young animal can distinguish between its parent and other members of its own species.

Exam tip

When considering human caregiver–infant interaction, make sure you can give one reason why research with non-human animals is useful and one reason why research with non-human animals is not useful.

Knowledge check 23

Suggest one difference between imprinting and attachment.

Explanations of attachment

Explanations of attachment try to account for how and why children become attached to a caregiver. You should learn these **two** theories of attachment: the learning theory explanation (behavioural) and Bowlby's theory of attachment.

The behavioural explanation (learning theory)

The basic principle of learning theory is that all behaviour is learned. The main argument proposed by behavioural theorists is that the infant's emotional dependence on, and bond with, his or her caregiver can be explained in terms of reinforcement arising from the satisfaction of basic physiological needs, such as food and drink. The mother (or caregiver) relieves these needs and thus acquires reward value as the infant learns to associate pleasure with the caregiver.

Based on **classical conditioning**, receiving food gives the infant pleasure, so when the caregiver feeds him or her, the infant feels pleasure. Thus an association is formed between the caregiver and food, so that whenever the caregiver is near, the infant feels pleasure — expressed as attachment behaviour.

Based on **operant conditioning**, infants feel discomfort when they are hungry and so desire food to remove the discomfort. They learn that if they cry, their caregiver feeds them and the discomfort is removed. This is **negative reinforcement**: the consequences of behaviour (crying) lead to something unpleasant ceasing (feeling hungry stops). Thus, proximity-seeking behaviour is reinforced, which in turn leads to the attachment behaviour of distress on being separated from the caregiver.

> ### Evaluation
>
> - Feeding cannot fully explain the development of attachments. Harlow's baby monkeys showed a preference for the cloth-covered mother, especially when they were distressed. This shows that attachment is not just about food. Harlow also found that, as adults, these monkeys found it difficult to form reproductive relationships and were poor mothers. This suggests that the lack of interaction with a caregiver may cause later maladjustment.

Bowlby's theory of attachment (1969)

Bowlby suggested that social behaviours, such as following, clinging, sucking, smiling and crying, are innate, and that the function of this behaviour is to bond the child to its caregiver. Bowlby suggested that infants are born with an innate drive to form attachments and that infants possess characteristics (**social releasers**, such as smiles) that facilitate the caregiver's attachment to them. According to Bowlby, attachment is an **interactive and innate two-way relationship**, in which the caregiver is as attached as the infant. The role of attachment is adaptive, as it promotes survival by (a) maintaining proximity (closeness) between infant and caregiver; (b) assisting cognitive development; and (c) providing the opportunity for learning through imitation.

Bowlby proposed that infants have many attachments but that the one at the top of the hierarchy has special significance for emotional development. The infant becomes

Exam tip

Make sure you can write a definition for the term **attachment**.

Knowledge check 24

Outline how behaviourist psychologists explain attachment.

most closely attached to the individual who responds in the most sensitive manner, which leads the infant to have one primary attachment object (**monotropy**). The primary attachment object need not be the infant's biological mother. The child learns from the relationship with the primary caregiver and this relationship acts as a **template** for future relationships. Bowlby called this an **internal working model** (a cognitive schema) that generates expectations for all future relationships.

Bowlby's attachment theory focuses on the interpersonal processes that create attachments, particularly the innate tendency in infants to seek attachment and to elicit caregiver responses through smiles and other social releasers. Bowlby proposed that the development of attachments follows an innate maturational sequence.

Phase 1: birth to 8 weeks

- Orientation and signals are directed towards people without discrimination.
- Infants behave in characteristic and friendly ways towards other people, but their ability to discriminate between them is limited.

Phase 2: 8–10 weeks to 6 months

- Orientation and signals are directed towards one or more special people.
- Infants continue to be generally friendly, but there is beginning to be a difference of behaviour towards one primary caregiver.

Phase 3: 6 months to 1–2 years old

- There is maintenance of closeness to a special person by means of locomotion as well as signals.
- The infant starts to follow his or her caregiver (displaying **separation anxiety**), greets the caregiver when he or she returns, and uses the caregiver as a safe base from which to explore.
- The infant selects other people as subsidiary attachment figures but treats strangers with caution (**stranger anxiety**).

Bowlby proposed that attachment between human infants and their caregivers is **adaptive behaviour** (evolutionary explanation). He suggested that there is a sensitive period that ends at around 1–3 years, during which infants develop a special attachment to one individual.

Factors that influence the development of attachments

Attachments are influenced by the following factors:

- **The age of the child.** Bowlby proposed that unless attachments have developed by between 1 and 3 years, they will not develop 'normally'.
- **The child's temperament.** Some aspects of temperament may be innate and a child's temperament may make it easier or harder for him or her to form attachments.
- **The quality of care.** Psychologists suggest that the sensitivity of the caregiver can also affect the development of attachments. Ainsworth et al. (1974) proposed that good, secure attachment is promoted by sensitive responsiveness from a caregiver and that attachment is related to the quality of the interactions between the infant and his or her caregiver. In support of this theory, Isabella et al. (1989) found that responsiveness in the mother towards a 1-month-old baby correlated with a close relationship between mother and baby at 1 year.

Knowledge check 25

Why is Bowlby's theory of attachment a 'nature' rather than a 'nurture' theory of attachment?

Exam tip

Make sure you can explain why attachment is *adaptive*.

Types of attachment

There are individual and cultural differences in styles of attachment. For example, some infants are **securely attached** whereas others are **insecurely attached**. Ainsworth and Bell (1970) developed the **strange situation** procedure to measure differences in infant attachment.

The strange situation (Ainsworth and Bell 1970)

The strange situation procedure involves controlled observation that allows researchers to assess how securely an infant is attached to a caregiver. It comprises seven episodes, each lasting about 3 minutes:

(1) The caregiver carries the infant into a room, puts the infant on the floor and then sits in a chair and does not interact with the infant unless the infant seeks attention.

(2) A stranger enters the room and talks with the caregiver, then approaches the infant with a toy.

(3) The caregiver leaves. If the infant plays, the stranger observes unobtrusively. If the infant is passive, the stranger tries to interest him or her in a toy. If the infant shows distress (crying), the stranger tries to comfort him or her.

(4) The caregiver returns and the stranger leaves.

(5) After the infant begins to play, the caregiver leaves and the infant is briefly left alone.

(6) The stranger re-enters the room and repeats the behaviour as described in step 3 above.

(7) The caregiver returns and the stranger leaves.

The strange situation procedure places the infant in a mildly stressful situation in order to observe four types of behaviour:

- **separation anxiety** — a securely attached child shows some anxiety but is fairly easily soothed
- **willingness to explore** — a securely attached child explores more when the caregiver is present
- **stranger anxiety** — the degree of security of attachment is related to the degree of stranger anxiety
- **reunion behaviour** — an insecurely attached infant may ignore the caregiver's return

Three attachment types

- **Secure attachment.** Securely attached infants show some anxiety when their caregiver departs but are easily soothed and greet the caregiver's return with enthusiasm. These infants play independently and return to the caregiver regularly for reassurance. Ainsworth et al. concluded that a secure attachment is associated with sensitivity in the caregiver, which teaches the infant to expect the same in other relationships. Secure attachment is generally related to healthy cognitive and emotional development, involving independence, self-confidence and trusting relationships.

Exam tip

You should be able to describe the procedure used in the strange situation and the four types of behaviour that are observed.

- **Insecure–avoidant attachment.** The infant shows indifference when the caregiver leaves, and does not display stranger anxiety. At reunion the infant actively avoids contact with the caregiver. The caregiver tends to be insensitive and may ignore the infant during play. These infants play independently.

- **Insecure–resistant attachment.** The infant is distressed when the caregiver goes and, although when the caregiver returns he or she rushes to the caregiver, the infant is not easily consoled. The infant may resist contact with the caregiver, or may seek comfort and reject it at the same time. These children explore less than other children. In samples of middle-class American children, Ainsworth et al. found that about 65% were classed as secure, 15% were classed as insecure–avoidant and 20% insecure–resistant.

Main and Solomon (1986) added a fourth type of attachment — **disorganised attachment** — in which there are no set patterns of behaviour at separation or reunion.

> **Knowledge check 26**
>
> Briefly describe how the behaviour of a securely attached infant differs from that of an insecurely attached infant.

How reliable is the strange situation?

Main et al. (1985) conducted a longitudinal study. Infants were assessed in the strange situation before the age of 18 months with both their mothers and fathers. When the children were retested at the age of 6 years, the researchers found considerable consistency in security of attachment to both parents. Of the secure babies, 100% were classified as securely attached to both parents at 6 years, and 75% of avoidant babies were reclassified as avoidant at age 6.

Cultural variation in attachment

If infant attachment is innate, then attachment behaviour should be similar in all cultures.

Sagi, van Ijzendoorn and Koren-Karie (1991) studied attachment styles of infants in the USA, Israel, Japan and Germany. They reported as follows:

- **American children** — 71% secure attachment, 12% insecure–resistant, 17% insecure–avoidant.
- **Israeli children** (raised in a kibbutz) — 62% secure attachment, 33% insecure–resistant, 5% insecure–avoidant. The children in the kibbutz were looked after by adults who were not their family, but they saw few strangers. This may explain why the children were not anxious when their caregiver left but were anxious when the stranger appeared.
- **Japanese children** — 68% secure attachment, 32% insecure–resistant and few insecure–avoidant. It was noted that Japanese children are rarely left by their mother, so the mother leaving during the strange situation may have been particularly stressful. Their anxious behaviour may be the result of the mother leaving rather than of a stranger arriving.
- **German children** — 40% securely attached, 49% insecure–avoidant, 11% insecure–resistant. German children are encouraged to be independent and not to be 'clingy'. The high percentage of insecure–avoidant children may reflect the cultural ethos of valuing independence.

Analysis of strange situation studies (van Ijzendoorn and Kroonenberg 1988)

The researchers compared the results of 32 strange situation studies in eight countries (involving 2,000 children).

Country	Number of studies	Percentage of each attachment type		
		Secure	Avoidant	Resistant
West Germany	3	57	35	8
Great Britain	1	75	22	3
Netherlands	4	67	26	7
Sweden	1	74	22	4
Israel	2	64	7	29
Japan	2	68	5	27
China	1	50	25	25
USA	18	65	21	14
Average		65	20	14

Criticisms: Variations within one culture were 1.5 times greater than variations between cultures, which suggests that any one culture may comprise several subcultures. Although large numbers of children were studied overall, some sample sizes were small. In the Chinese study, for example, only 36 children were used and it may be unsafe to generalise the results to all Chinese infants as 36 children may not be representative of the population. The strange situation is based on US culture and observed behaviour may not have the same meaning in different cultures. The use of procedures developed in one culture may not be a valid measure of behaviour in another culture.

Disruption of attachment

In developmental psychology:

- **Separation** is when a child is separated from his or her attachment figure for a relatively short period of time.
- **Deprivation** is the loss of something that is needed. Maternal deprivation occurs when a child has formed an attachment but then experiences the loss of the mother or other attachment figure. The loss is long term or permanent and the attachment bond is broken.
- **Privation** means never having been able to satisfy a certain need. Maternal privation is when a child has never been able to form a close relationship (develop an attachment) with any one caregiver.

Maternal deprivation: Bowlby's maternal deprivation hypothesis

Bowlby (1953) proposed that long-term maternal deprivation — the loss of the mother figure or other attachment figure — is harmful: 'Mother love in infancy and childhood is as important for mental health as are vitamins and proteins for physical health' (Bowlby 1951).

Exam tip

If, as Bowlby suggests, infant attachment is innate, then attachment behaviour should be similar in all cultures. You should be able to explain how the findings of cross-cultural research can be used to suggest whether or not attachment is innate.

Bowlby suggested that continuous 'maternal care' is necessary for emotional and cognitive development (maternal care may be provided by a 'mother substitute'). This is a 'critical period' hypothesis because, according to Bowlby, there is a critical period, before the age of 2½, during which maternal deprivation will affect development and the effects will be permanent.

In sum, deprivation of the primary caregiver during the critical period has harmful effects on the child's emotional, social and cognitive development. The long-term effects may include separation anxiety expressed as 'clingy behaviour' and reluctance to attend school, and future relationships may be affected by emotional insecurity.

Maternal privation and effects of institutionalism

Maternal privation is when a child has never been able to develop an attachment to his or her mother or another caregiver.

Rutter (1981) argued that the term 'maternal deprivation' is misleading because 'deprivation' refers to a variety of different experiences and outcomes. He also argued that even when separation is related to psychosocial problems, this does not mean that separation causes poor development, and that affectionless psychopathy may be the result of an initial failure to develop attachments, rather than a result of broken attachments. This is the distinction between privation (a lack of attachments) and deprivation (a loss of attachments).

Exam tip

Make sure you know the difference between separation, deprivation and privation.

Case studies of maternal privation

Genie: Curtiss (1989)

Genie was discovered at the age of 13. She had been kept in one room, isolated, beaten and malnourished. Although she was given extensive education, and her perceptual skills were reported to be near normal, her language skills did not develop normally. As she grew up, she had a series of difficult relationships with carers.

The Koluchova twins (Koluchova 1976, 1991)

The researcher studied twin boys who had been locked in a cellar and who had suffered extreme privation until the age of 7. When found, the children had virtually no language skills. When they were 9, they were fostered in a loving home. By the age of 14 their behaviour and intellect were normal. By the age of 20 they were described as of above average intelligence and having loving relationships with members of their foster family.

The concentration camp children (Freud and Dann 1951)

The researchers studied six orphans who had spent their first 3 years, without continuous adult care, in a concentration camp. They were strongly attached to each other and were afraid of being separated. At first they were hostile towards adults, but eventually they developed normal social and cognitive skills. As adults they were described as being within the 'normal range' of development.

Evaluation

Although these are all case studies, which make it impossible to generalise, the differences between the cases are important. The following factors should be considered:

- duration of privation (Genie's was the longest)
- experiences during privation (the Koluchova twins had each other for company, as did the concentration camp children; Genie suffered physical, social and emotional abuse, was alone and was not placed in a loving foster home)
- quality of care following privation (the twins were adopted but Genie was passed between academic psychologists as a research interest and then placed in an institution)
- individual differences in the temperament and intellect of the child

Exam tip

You need to be able to explain the advantages and limitations of the case study method.

Knowledge check 27

Define maternal privation.

A key study on maternal privation: Hodges and Tizard (1989)

Hodges and Tizard (1989) looked at whether there is a critical (or sensitive) period in which failure to make a secure attachment can be shown to affect adult relationships. They studied a group of children from their early days in an institution (children's home) until they were 16 years old. Some of the children were adopted and experienced 'normal' emotional attachments. This enabled the researchers to observe whether early privation was associated with long-term emotional damage.

Sixty-five children were studied. The children had been placed in an institution before they were 4 months old. The 'home' had a policy against the 'caretakers' forming attachments to the children and, before the age of 4, the children had had an average of 50 different caretakers. Thus the children (and caretakers) were unlikely to have formed any specific attachments.

By the age of 4, 24 of the institutionalised children had been adopted, 15 had returned to their natural homes (the 'restored' group) and the rest remained in the institution. The children were assessed then, and again when they were 8 years old, at which time the sample was reduced to 51 children.

By the time the children reached the age of 16, the researchers were able to locate and interview 23 of the adopted children (some of whom had been adopted after the age of 4), 11 'restored' children and 5 children who had remained in institutions. A comparison (control) group, consisting of children matched for age and gender with the children in the sample, was established.

The emotional adjustment of the children was assessed using interviews and questionnaires conducted with the children, their matched controls, their parents or caretakers and their teachers. The data collected concerned attitudes and behaviour.

Findings at age 16 were as follows:

- **Relationships within the family.** The adopted children were as closely attached to their parents as the comparison group, whereas the restored group was much less likely to be closely attached. Restored children were reportedly less cuddly, harder to give affection to, and less involved with their families.

- **Peer relationships.** All the ex-institution adolescents were less likely to have a special friend, to be part of a crowd or to be liked by other children. They were more quarrelsome and more likely to be bullies.
- **Other adults outside the family.** The ex-institution children were more attention seeking and the restored children were more aggressive.
- **Summary.** The comparison and adopted children were most similar in terms of relationships within the family. In relationships with peers and with adults outside the family, the adopted and restored ex-institution children were most similar.

Five possible explanations can be offered for the results:

- The adopted families were more middle class than the restored families — was there a class-related difference?
- Perhaps the adopted children suffered from poor self-esteem because they were adopted, which affected their relationships outside the home.
- Adoptive parents put a lot of effort into relationships between themselves and their children but not between the children and their peers. This would explain why the adopted children had good relationships with parents but not with their peers. Restored children had no special help with any relationships, which explains why they had difficulty in all relationships.
- Perhaps the ability to form peer relationships is especially affected by early emotional deprivation. Therefore, the adopted children were able to recover their family relationships when given good emotional care, but the same did not happen for their peer relationships.
- Perhaps the ex-institutional children lag behind their peers in emotional development.

Romanian orphan studies

In 1989 the Ceausescu regime in Romania was overthrown. There were thousands of babies and children in orphanages, many of whom had suffered severe emotional and physical deprivation.

Rutter studied children who had been adopted after having lived with deprivation or privation. Initial findings showed that the children had poor health and also had behaviour issues such as temper tantrums, excessive rocking, insomnia and indiscriminate friendliness. He compared 111 Romanian children who were adopted in England before they were 2 years old with 52 other children of similar ages adopted within England. Rutter found that, on adoption, the Romanian children had poor physical health and an average IQ of 63. When these children were assessed again the average IQ for those adopted before the age of 6 months had gone from 63 to 107, but for those adopted after the age of 6 months the average IQ had only increased from 45 to 90. Rutter also studied attachment. Some of the Romanian children continued to experience serious behavioural problems both in general and when it came to the issue of forming a bond with their adoptive parents.

Another study conducted in Canada looked at similar Romanian orphans adopted by Canadian families. This study involved three separate groups of children:

- Group 1: Canadian children who had not been adopted
- Group 2: Romanian children whose median age was 18½ months
- Group 3: Romanian children who were adopted before they reached 4 months old

Exam tip

Make sure you can explain why the study by Hodges and Tizard is a study of maternal privation.

Knowledge check 28

Hodges and Tizard found that the adopted children formed good relationships with their families but not with their peers. Give one explanation for this finding.

Exam tip

The studies of Romanian orphans are longitudinal research. You could be asked to explain one advantage of using longitudinal research to study child development.

The researchers found no difference in the attachments formed by children in groups 1 and 3. Group 2 however had attachment difficulties, although most eventually formed attachments with their adoptive parents. The conclusion was that the longer children are institutionalised, the harder it becomes for them to form attachments.

The influence of early attachment on childhood and adult relationships

The role of an internal working model

Based on Freud's idea that the mother–child relationship acts as a prototype for all future attachments, Bowlby believed that an attachment creates an internal working model (a cognitive schema) for all future relationships and that this first attachment forms a template or schema that gives the child a feel for what a relationship is. An internal working model is a set of expectations and beliefs about the self, others and the relationship between the self and others. Thus, the internal working model of an individual will contain particular expectations and beliefs about:

- my own and other people's behaviour
- whether or not I am loveable and worthy of love
- whether or not others will help and support me

Internal working models begin to be formed in early infancy. If a baby finds that his feelings of hunger and his crying behaviour result in a prompt response from a loving adult he learns that he is loved and nurtured and that he 'deserves' this response. At the other end of the spectrum, a response that is unavailable or cold will lead to an internal working model of the attachment figure as rejecting, the self as unworthy of care and others as not to be relied on for help and support. Children's behaviours become organised around their expectations of themselves and others and these expectations tend to influence the way in which others relate to them. For example, the young person who feels good about herself and expects others to be mostly warm and friendly will present herself to a potential new friendship group in a way that signals, 'I will be a good friend' and so elicits a positive response. Conversely, a young person who expects rejection or has low self-esteem is likely to signal, 'I don't need or want your friendship, don't come close to me', which tends to bring about further rejection.

The internal working model is used in future years to develop other relationships and is particularly important in determining parenting skills in later life. For example, a secure attachment as a child leads to greater emotional and social stability as an adult, whereas an insecure attachment is likely to lead to difficulties with later relationships and is likely to be reflected in the parenting style when the child matures and has children of his or her own.

Attachment: glossary of terms

attachment: a strong emotional bond that develops over time between an infant and his or her primary caregiver(s), resulting in a desire to maintain proximity. The attachment bond is thought to form the basis of emotional development and long-term adult relationships.

Exam tip

In the exam you could be given a hypothetical case study of a child who has been in some way 'institutionalised' and be asked to explain the child's behaviour with reference to Bowlby's theory of maternal deprivation.

Knowledge check 29

'The mother–child relationship acts as a prototype for future attachments.' Referring to the 'internal working model' explain what this quote means.

deprivation: in terms of attachment, deprivation refers to the experience of attachment bond disruption as a result of separation from the attachment figure for a period of time. Note that if there is no bond disruption, then separation not deprivation has occurred.

insecure attachment: a form of attachment which is not optimal for healthy development. Two examples of insecure attachment are avoidant and resistant attachment. Avoidant attachment is shown in the 'strange situation' by indifference when the caregiver leaves, little stranger anxiety and avoidance of contact with the caregiver when he or she returns.

interactional synchrony: the behaviour of caregivers and infants who 'move in time' with each other and who appear to take turns communicating.

internal working model: an attachment creates an internal working model (a cognitive schema) for all future relationships and the first attachment forms a template or schema that gives the child a feel for what a relationship is.

maternal deprivation hypothesis: the suggestion (Bowlby) that separation from a primary caregiver, and thus the breaking of the attachment bond, has long-term negative effects on emotional development.

privation: a lack of any attachment bonds, which may lead to permanent emotional damage.

reciprocity: during caregiver–infant interaction, reciprocal behaviour is behaviour that is produced as a response to the behaviour of another person or behaviour that is produced to elicit a response from another person.

secure attachment: a form of attachment which is optimal for healthy cognitive and emotional development. The securely attached infant is able to function independently because its caregiver provides a secure base. In the 'strange situation', the infant is upset when the caregiver departs but greets him or her positively when the caregiver returns, and is quickly soothed.

Knowledge summary

You should be able to:
- define examples of caregiver–infant interactions
- describe and evaluate the learning theory of attachment
- describe and evaluate Bowlby's explanation of attachment
- describe the characteristics of three types of attachment: secure attachment, insecure-avoidant and insecure-resistant
- describe the procedures used in the 'strange situation'
- explain how the 'strange situation' is used in attachment research
- describe research into cultural variations in attachment
- explain how attachment creates an internal working model
- explain the effects of disruption of attachment and differentiate between disruption of attachment and privation
- describe research into the failure to form attachment (privation)
- describe and evaluate research into the effect of institutional care

■ Psychopathology

This topic is examined on AS Paper 2 and on A-level Paper 1.

In this topic you must understand and be able to describe how psychologists define abnormality, including statistical infrequency, deviation from social norms, a failure to function adequately and deviation from ideal mental health. You also need to be able to describe and evaluate approaches to psychological illness, including the behavioural, cognitive and biological approaches.

Definitions of abnormality

Abnormality as behaviour that deviates from the statistical norm

Some psychologists propose that behaviour is normally distributed. If this is true, then people whose behaviour is different (more than two standard deviations above or below the mean) can be defined as 'abnormal'.

Evaluation

- This approach accounts for the frequency of behaviour, not its desirability. A low IQ is, statistically, just as abnormal as a high IQ, but it is desirable to have a high IQ. Therefore, frequency of behaviour tells us nothing about its desirability.
- It does not allow us to distinguish between rare behaviour that is eccentric (elective), such as keeping snails as pets, and rare behaviour that is psychologically abnormal, such as schizophrenia.
- It is difficult to define the point at which normal behaviour becomes abnormal behaviour. For example, at what point on the distribution curve does a person's IQ become abnormal?
- Some behaviour, such as depressive illness, is psychologically abnormal but is not that rare.

Abnormality as behaviour that deviates from the social norm

Some people behave in socially deviant ways. Because their behaviour does not fit in with social norms or meet social expectations, they are seen as different. For example, a person who scavenges in dustbins and hoards rubbish in their home may be seen as abnormal.

Evaluation

- This definition could be used to discriminate against people who the majority disapprove of and want to remove from society. For example, in the UK in the early part of the twentieth century, unmarried girls who became pregnant could be diagnosed as mentally ill and locked in asylums.
- Whether behaviour is seen as normal depends on its context. Preaching a sermon is seen as normal in a church, but preaching a sermon in a supermarket might be considered abnormal.
- Social norms and attitudes change. Homosexuality was believed to be a mental illness until the 1970s but is not seen as such today.
- Social norms vary within and between cultures; there is not one universally acceptable set of social norms. In Muslim countries, a woman who dressed provocatively in public would be viewed as socially deviant, but this behaviour is common among women in Western society.

Abnormality as failure to function adequately

People who cannot look after themselves or who are perceived to be irrational or out of control are often described as abnormal. The problem with this is that it involves others in making value judgements about what it means to function adequately. The individuals themselves may not think they have a problem and their unusual behaviour may be a way of coping with their difficulties in life.

Abnormality as deviation from ideal mental health

Jahoda (1958) identified six conditions associated with ideal mental health:

(1) a positive self-attitude and high self-esteem

(2) a drive to realise self-potential (personal growth)

(3) the ability to cope with stress

(4) being in control and making your own decisions (personal autonomy)

(5) an accurate perception of reality and the ability to feel for others

(6) the ability to adapt to changes in one's environment

> **Exam tip**
>
> In the exam you could be given a description of a fictitious person's behaviour and asked to apply the definitions of abnormality to explain why the behaviour might be judged to be abnormal.

Evaluation

- The degree to which a person meets the six criteria may vary over time. Thus, the degree to which any individual can be defined as 'normal' might vary from day to day.
- It is a subjective standard — it is difficult to measure self-esteem and self-potential.
- It is an ethnocentric standard — it describes normality from an individualistic rather than from a collectivist cultural standpoint.
- By this standard, it is possible that most people could be defined as abnormal.

> **Knowledge check 30**
>
> Give two definitions of psychological abnormality.

Behavioural, emotional and cognitive characteristics of phobias, depression and OCD

Phobic disorders

Phobias are a form of anxiety disorder in which the emotional response to an often harmless object (e.g. spider) has become chronic and disabling fear. Phobias consist of irrational fears that are out of proportion to the reality of the threat provided by the fear-provoking stimulus.

- **Physical symptoms:** the body's response to stress, such as breathlessness and tightness in the chest, hyperventilation (increased breathing) and palpitations (increased heart rate).
- **Behavioural symptoms:** avoidance behaviour is shown as the individual usually avoids the feared object, which can restrict his or her everyday behaviour.
- **Emotional symptoms:** anxiety is accompanied by a feeling of dread. The individual is frightened and distressed and may feel he or she is about to die or lose control of bodily functions.
- **Cognitive symptoms:** anxiety can decrease concentration and so decrease the person's ability to perform complex tasks. Reduced cognitive capacity can inhibit workplace functioning.
- **Social symptoms:** anxiety may reduce the individual's ability to cope with social settings and so inhibit personal and social functioning.

Diagnostic criteria: those who suffer from phobic disorders:

- have a persistent fear of a specific object or situation
- have a rapid anxiety response when exposed to the fear-provoking stimulus
- recognise that the fear experienced is excessive
- either avoid the phobic stimulus or respond to it with great anxiety
- find the phobic reactions interfere with their working or social life

Examples of phobic disorders

- **Social phobia:** social phobia is a fear of social situations due to self-consciousness about one's own behaviour and fear of others' reactions. This can be *generalised*, where the individual suffers social anxiety in most situations, or *specific* where the individual fears a particular situation, such as public speaking. The prevalence is 8% of the population, 70% of which are female.
- **Agoraphobia:** this is the fear of open or public places, which can include open or closed spaces, public transport, or crowds. Approximately 50% of all phobics suffer with agoraphobia with panic disorder. The prevalence is 3–4% of the population, and 75% are female.

Obsessive compulsive disorder (OCD)

OCD is a severe anxiety disorder thought to affect around 1–3% of the population (source: National Institute of Mental Health). OCD affects both men and women equally.

- **Physical symptoms:** the body's response to stress, such as breathlessness and tightness in the chest, hyperventilation (increased breathing) and palpitations (increased heart rate).
- **Behavioural symptoms:** compulsive behaviour — the irresistible urge to carry out repetitive behaviour to avoid some form of danger.
- **Emotional symptoms:** anxiety and depression — OCD can last from a few years to decades and sufferers can go through intermittent periods of depression.
- **Cognitive symptoms:** obsession is the persistent and recurrent thoughts and images which enter the mind and cannot be removed.

Diagnostic criteria: those who suffer from OCD:
- acknowledge the problem but are powerless to overcome it
- suffer from severe anxiety (leading to symptoms)
- suffer from severe depression (i.e. a symptom)
- experience the onset in late teens/early 20s
- experience either obsession or compulsion
- find obsessions and/or compulsions time consuming in the daily routine

Examples of OCD
- **Obsessional cleanliness:** obsession with dirt/contamination that leads to compulsive behaviours, e.g. hand-washing.
- **Compulsive rituals:** specific ways/order of doing things.
- **Compulsive checking:** have to keep checking, double-checking things, e.g. the house door.

Depression (unipolar)

Depression is a mood disorder in which a negative emotional state colours a person's thoughts and behaviour. Clinical depression occurs when depression lasts a long time and affects a person's ability to function normally. Depressive illness is the cause of more than 25% of all deaths by suicide.
- **Physical symptoms:** aches and pains, lack of energy, loss of weight and appetite.
- **Behavioural symptoms:** sufferers stop socialising, lose interest in sex, may attempt suicide, daily activities take longer to complete.
- **Emotional symptoms:** feelings of sadness and despair, and absence of feeling, little or no interest in everyday activities.
- **Cognitive symptoms:** memory and concentration are affected, sufferers think negatively and may think about committing suicide, also persistent worrying.

Diagnostic criteria: diagnosis requires five or more symptoms, including for at least 2 weeks:
- extreme sadness
- tearfulness
- depressed mood
- loss of interest in, and pleasure in, usual activities as well as social withdrawal

Exam tip

In an exam you may be given a description of the symptoms of a fictitious person and asked to suggest a diagnosis.

Exam tip

You could be asked to outline the cognitive and behavioural characteristics of a phobia, OCD or depression.

Knowledge check 31

Freddie washes his hands then washes them again. He isn't sure they are clean so he washes them again. He dries his hands on the towel — but then worries that the towel may not be clean so he washes his hands again. This compulsive behaviour is a symptom of which anxiety disorder?

The behavioural approach to explaining and treating phobias

Explaining phobias

The behavioural approach makes **three assumptions**. First, it assumes that all behaviour is learned; second, that what has been learned can be unlearned; and third, that abnormal behaviour is learned in the same way as normal behaviour. This model sees the abnormal behaviour as the problem and not a symptom of an underlying cause.

Behaviourists propose that **classical conditioning** can explain phobias. In classical conditioning, an unconditioned stimulus, such as an unexpected loud noise, triggers a natural reflex, e.g. the startle response and fear. But, if another stimulus, e.g. seeing a spider, occurs at the same time, this may in future elicit the fear response. Watson and Rayner (1920) demonstrated how classical conditioning could explain the way in which fear could be learned.

Behaviourists also propose that abnormal behaviour can be learned by the process of **operant conditioning**, in which behaviour is learned through the consequences of our actions. If our actions result in rewarding consequences (positive reinforcement), or in something nasty ceasing (negative reinforcement), we will repeat the behaviour, but we will not repeat behaviour that has bad outcomes. Phobias such as fear of heights can be learned in this way. We become anxious at the thought of climbing the ladder, so we employ a window cleaner in order to avoid using a ladder, and this removes the anxiety (negative reinforcement).

Classical conditioning (learning by association)

We learn by associating things. Pavlov's dogs learned to associate a bell with food so that eventually the sound of the bell alone would cause the dogs to salivate. Little Albert learned to associate a white rat with loud and frightening noises so that after a few days anything white and furry would evoke a fear response. This approach offers a simple and testable theory of learning and offers an explanation for phobias. However, Menzies and Clark (1993) reported that only 2% of children who had hydrophobia had suffered a traumatic event involving water. Also, the behaviourist approach cannot explain why phobias for some objects are more common than others. Many objects are far more threatening than spiders and snakes and Seligman believes we have a genetic predisposition to associate fear with some threats based on our more primitive past.

Operant conditioning (reward and punishment)

If we are rewarded for behaviour we are more likely to repeat it. If we are punished we are less likely to do it again. Abnormal behaviour is therefore caused by people reinforcing inappropriate behaviour, making it more likely to be repeated. For example, a panic attack gets a child attention, making it likely to be repeated.

Social learning theory (modelling)

Behaviourists also propose that we acquire behaviour by copying others and that observers are more likely to copy the behaviour they see if the models are rewarded for their behaviour (e.g. Bandura's Bobo doll study). Mineka et al. (1994) showed

> **Knowledge check 32**
>
> Milly has a phobia of spiders. Can you explain how the processes of classical and operant conditioning are both involved in the learning of this phobia?

monkeys video footage of other monkeys who were clearly frightened of snakes. When exposed to snakes it was found that the observer monkeys had also developed a fear of snakes.

The two-process model

The learning and maintenance of a phobia involves both classical and operant conditioning:

- Classical conditioning because the fear is first learned by association.
- Operant conditioning because avoiding the fear-provoking stimulus prevents us from unlearning the fear, which explains why a phobia persists.

For example, at a young age you are in the garden and a butterfly gets in your hair. Your sister screams and this frightens you. You have learned to associate butterflies with being frightened. To unlearn this fear you need to associate butterflies with something pleasant, but you avoid butterflies which is reinforcing because it prevents anxiety — as a result you remain frightened of butterflies.

Treating phobias

Since the abnormal behaviour has been learned then treatment concentrates on unlearning inappropriate behaviour and replacing it with the learning of new behaviours. Behaviour therapies (based on classical conditioning) are often used to treat phobias and involve patients learning to associate their phobic stimulus (e.g. snake) with relaxation.

Systematic desensitisation

This is a type of behaviour therapy where the undesired behaviour, for instance a person's phobia, is broken down into the small stimulus–response units that comprise it. The patient is taught a muscle relaxation technique and breathing exercises. The patient creates a **fear hierarchy** starting at stimuli that create the least anxiety and building up in stages to fear-provoking images. Patients work their way up starting at the least unpleasant and practising their relaxation technique as they go. The role of the therapist is to help the patient recognise the reason for the fear, and whether the fear is rational or not and to help the patient as the fear is unlearned. Systematic desensitisation is an effective therapy. Patients show much greater recovery than with no therapy.

The therapy therefore consists of:
- the construction of a hierarchy of fears
- training in relaxation — the relaxed state is incompatible with anxiety
- graded exposure (in imagination) and relaxation
- homework — practice in real life

For instance in a phobia of snakes, the least stressful situation might be to look at a picture of a snake and the most stressful might be to have to touch a snake. The therapist works though each S–R unit in the ascending hierarchy, helping the person to replace each dysfunctional response of being afraid, with the response of feeling relaxed. **McGrath et al. (1990)** reported that, following systematic desensitisation, 70% of patients showed improvement in symptoms, but few patients were completely free of anxiety.

Knowledge check 33

Briefly explain how systematic desensitisation may be used to treat a phobia.

Flooding (exposure therapy)

In flooding the patient is confronted with his or her phobic stimulus. The theory is that the person suffers panic, but because the adrenaline response (fight or flight response) is short lived soon the person calms due to lack of adrenaline. Exposure therapy seems to be more effective than systematic desensitisation and does not involve muscle relaxation.

Exam tip

Make a list of the differences between classical and operant conditioning.

Evaluation

Strengths
- The behavioural approach proposes a simple testable explanation that is supported by experimental evidence.
- The behavioural approach is hopeful as it predicts that people can change (re-learn) their behaviour.

Limitations
- The approach is criticised as being dehumanising and mechanistic (Heather 1976). People are reduced to programmed stimulus–response units.
- The approach cannot explain all psychological disorders. Conditioning cannot cure disorders, e.g. schizophrenia.

Knowledge check 34

Outline the assumptions of the behavioural approach to abnormality.

The cognitive approach to explaining and treating depression

Explaining depression

The cognitive approach to depression assumes that the human mind is like an information processor and that people can control how they select, store and think about information. In the cognitive approach, psychological problems are caused when people make incorrect inferences about themselves or others, and have negative thoughts about themselves and the future.

Beck and Clark (1988) found that irrational beliefs were common in patients suffering anxiety and depression. For example, depressive people often believe that they are unloved, that they are failures as parents, and that nothing good will ever happen in the future.

The cognitive approach explains depression in terms of an overly pessimistic outlook on life. Beck (1967) for example describes the 'cognitive triad' in which depressed patients have a negative view of themselves, the world and the future. The cognitive approach views the symptoms as the causes of depression.

Ellis (1962) suggests that faulty perceptions were due to 'mustabation' (e.g. 'I must get grade As or I'll be seen as stupid) and 'awfulising' (e.g. 'I didn't get invited to the party so no one likes me'). The cognitive model has been successful in explaining and treating depression arising from negative thinking.

Ellis' ABC model (1962)

A: activating agent (e.g. getting a grade B in an exam)

B: belief which can be rational (e.g. grade B is good enough) or irrational (e.g. grade B is a disaster)

C: consequence which can be healthy (e.g. bank grade B and feel relieved) or unhealthy (e.g. worry that you will fail next exam)

Beck's cognitive triad

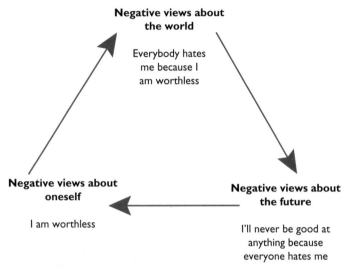

Negative views about the world

Everybody hates me because I am worthless

Negative views about oneself

I am worthless

Negative views about the future

I'll never be good at anything because everyone hates me

Figure 5 Beck's cognitive triad

Beck believes patients get drawn into a negative pattern of viewing themselves, the world and the future. Combined with negative schemas and cognitive biases these produce an inescapable cycle of negative thoughts. Beck believes that a depressed person has developed a negative set of schemas upon which his or her expectations about life are based. For example, depressed people may have developed a self-blame schema which makes them feel responsible for all the things in their life that go wrong. Depressed people also overgeneralise, drawing negative conclusions about all situations based on one, perhaps trivial event. For example, not being invited to a party convinces the person that he or she has no friends and that no one will ever like him or her.

> **Exam tip**
>
> You may be given a description of a fictitious person's irrational thought processes and asked to apply Beck's cognitive triad to explain why these thought processes are damaging.

Treating depression

A number of cognitive therapies have become popular. They all work in a similar way. First, getting patients to recognise their irrational perceptions, then agreeing on a more realistic approach and finally putting this into practice in a real-life situation.

> **Knowledge check 35**
>
> Look at the diagram of Beck's cognitive triad. Draw and label the diagram from memory.

Cognitive behaviour therapy (CBT)

CBT recognises the importance of changing both behaviour and thinking. The assumptions underlying CBT are:

- It is our interpretation of events rather than the events themselves that is important.
- Thoughts, behaviours and feelings all influence each other.
- The role of the therapist is to help patients identify their irrational thoughts and to change their interpretations of themselves and to get rid of negative biases.
- Patients must change both their thinking and their behaviour.

Butler et al. (2006) studied the results from over 10,000 patients and found that CBT was effective in treating depression (more successfully than anti-depressives), anxiety disorder, panic disorder and social phobia.

Evaluation

Strengths

- The cognitive approach focuses on how the individual experiences the world and on his or her feelings and beliefs rather than relying on interpretations by other people.
- The approach is hopeful as it assumes people have the power to change their behaviour.

Limitations

- The approach may encourage the idea that people are responsible for their own psychological problems, i.e. that they can be 'normal' if they want to. This could lead to people being blamed for psychological abnormalities.
- The approach is reductionist, as it ignores biological causes of psychological abnormality such as genetics and biochemistry.

Knowledge check 36

Outline how a cognitive psychologist would explain depression.

The biological approach to explaining and treating OCD

Explaining OCD

Biological approaches to psychopathology explore differences caused by genetics, biochemistry and brain anatomy. The biological approach assumes that psychological abnormalities such as OCD are symptoms of underlying physical causes.

Genetic explanation

Research suggests that OCD runs in families. **Murphy (2003)** looked for variations of the human serotonin transporter gene which controls the movement of the chemical between nerve cells in the brain. DNA was taken from 170 people; 30 had OCD. Murphy found that six out of seven people in two separate families who had one gene mutation had an OCD and the four people with the most severe OCD symptoms also had a second mutation in the same gene. **Carey and Gottesman (1981)** reported a prevalence of up to 10% in first-degree relatives. **Lenane (1990)** found that 30% of first-degree relatives also had an OCD. In a twin study, **Hoaker and Schnurr (1980)** found a concordance rate of 50–60%.

Neural (biochemical) explanation

OCD may result from a deficiency of serotonin (neurotransmitter) or a malfunction of its metabolism like blocked serotonin receptors. **Zohar et al. (1996)** found that some tricyclic drugs that inhibit the reuptake of serotonin were beneficial for around 60% of OCD sufferers, but **Lydiard et al. (1996)** found that drugs only provided partial alleviation from the symptoms.

Treating OCD: drug therapy

Anti-anxiety (anxiolytic) drugs such as benzodiazepines slow the activity of the central nervous system (CNS), reducing serotonin activity and thus anxiety, and increasing relaxation. Beta blockers act on the autonomic nervous system (ANS) to reduce activity in the ANS associated with anxiety — these drugs reduce heart rate, blood pressure and levels of cortisol. Antidepressant drugs, such as Prozac, can be used to elevate mood. Selective serotonin reuptake inhibitor (SSRI) drugs reduce symptoms of OCD and these SSRI drugs are the main treatment for OCD (e.g. Prozac). SSRI drugs increase levels of the neurotransmitter serotonin and are an effective treatment for anxiety disorders.

Knowledge check 37

Explain the **physiological effect** of one drug used to treat OCD.

Evaluation

Strengths

- Biological therapies (drugs) act rapidly to reduce the symptoms of OCD so that patients can lead a normal life.
- Drug therapy can be used alongside CBT.
- Drug treatments are easy to administer and do not involve patients changing their lifestyle or behaviour.

Limitations

- Biological therapies may give rise to ethical concerns. Some drug therapies can have unpleasant side effects.
- Taking drugs may lead to addiction and dependency.
- Drugs may simply suppress the symptoms, not cure the disorder.
- CBT is also an effective treatment for OCD. This contradicts the neural (serotonin) theory.

Knowledge check 38

Outline the neural explanation for OCD.

Exam tip

In an exam you could be asked to evaluate the biological explanation for OCD. Make sure you can list two strengths and two limitations of this explanation.

Approaches to psychopathology: a comparison

Approach	Where problems originate	Criticism	Comment
Biological Abnormality is a symptom of an underlying biological cause: biology of brain, genes etc.	Inside the person. It may be: ■ inherited/genetic ■ brain damage ■ abnormal neurotransmission	Deterministic. Reductionist. No free will. Can't explain why talking cures or conditioning are effective.	Ignores psychosocial factors but is scientific. Does not 'blame' the individual. Treatment = **drugs**
Behavioural Abnormal behaviour is learned and can be unlearned. Abnormal behaviour should be removed and/or treated.	Abnormal behaviour is learned in interaction with the environment: ■ classical or operant conditioning ■ stimulus–response learning	Deterministic/the past. No free will. Can't explain why drugs or talking cures work.	Ignores biological factors. Does not 'blame' the individual. Treatment based on conditioning (learning).
Cognitive Abnormality is caused by mental processes not functioning properly.	Inside the person: ■ irrational thoughts ■ negative thinking, e.g. depression, 'awfulising'	May 'blame' the individual: if you didn't think irrationally you wouldn't have a problem! Can't explain why drug treatment is effective.	Ignores biological and social factors. Treatment = **talking cure, CBT**.

Psychopathology: glossary of terms

abnormality: a psychological condition, or behaviour, that differs from how most people behave and that is harmful, or which causes distress to the individual or those around them. Abnormal behaviour is behaviour that does not match society's idea of what is appropriate.

behavioural approach to abnormality: an approach that sees the abnormal behaviour as the problem rather than as the symptom of an underlying cause. It makes three assumptions: first, that all behaviour is learned; second, that what has been learned can be unlearned; and third, that abnormal behaviour is learned in the same way as normal behaviour.

biological approach to abnormality: an approach that assumes that psychological abnormalities are symptoms of underlying physical causes.

classical conditioning: treatment, based on the behavioural approach, in which an undesirable behaviour can be paired with an unpleasant response (aversion therapy).

cognitive approach to abnormality: an approach that proposes that to be normal is to be able to use cognitive processes to monitor and control our behaviour. By this view, abnormal behaviour is caused by faulty or irrational thoughts, or when people make incorrect inferences about themselves or others, and/or about themselves and the future.

depression: a mood disorder.

deviation from ideal mental health: abnormality is seen as a deviation from an ideal of positive mental health, when ideal mental health includes having a positive attitude towards oneself, resistance to stress and an accurate perception of reality.

deviation from social norms: abnormal behaviour is seen as a deviation from the implicit rules about how one 'ought' to behave, where any behaviour that does not 'fit in' with these social rules is considered to be abnormal.

drug therapy: treatment based on the biological approach, which assumes that an imbalance in biochemistry (neurotransmitters) is the cause of the abnormality. Drug treatments may include anti-anxiety drugs, such as benzodiazepines, to slow the activity of the central nervous system (CNS), reducing serotonin activity and thus anxiety. Antipsychotic drugs can be used to reduce mental confusion and delusions. Antidepressant drugs, such as Prozac, can be used to treat OCD and depression.

failure to function adequately: if behaviour interferes with how people function in their everyday lives, for instance being unable to care for themselves, the behaviour is seen as abnormal.

OCD: obsessive compulsive disorder — an anxiety disorder.

phobia: an irrational fear — an anxiety disorder.

statistical infrequency: abnormality is defined as any behaviour that is rare.

systematic desensitisation: treatment based on the behavioural approach in which a person having a phobia can be gradually reintroduced to a feared object or situation.

Knowledge summary

You should be able to:
- describe definitions of abnormality, including deviation from social norms, failure to function adequately and deviation from ideal mental health
- evaluate these definitions of psychological abnormality
- describe and evaluate the behavioural, emotional and cognitive characteristics of phobias, depression and obsessive compulsive disorders (OCD)

- describe and evaluate the behavioural approach to explaining and treating phobias
- describe and evaluate the cognitive approach to explaining and treating depression
- describe and evaluate the biological approach to explaining and treating OCD

Questions & Answers

This section contains 16 questions: four on social influence, four on memory, four on attachment and four on psychopathology. Unless otherwise stated, the example questions can be used as practice questions for both AS Paper 1 (or in the case of psychopathology AS Paper 2) and A-level Paper 1.

The section is structured as follows:

- sample questions in the style of the exam
- example student responses at grade A/B (student A), demonstrating thorough knowledge, good understanding and an ability to deal with the data presented in the question
- example student responses at grade C/D (student B), demonstrating strengths and weaknesses and the potential for improvement

Exam advice

All example responses are followed by exam advice, preceded by the icon **e**. These comments may indicate where credit is due, strengths in the answer, areas for improvement, specific problems, common errors, lack of clarity, irrelevance, mistakes in the meaning of terms and/or misinterpretation of the question. Comments indicate how the answers might be marked in an exam. Some questions are also followed by a brief analysis of what to watch out for when answering them (shown by the icon **e**).

Exam format

If you are studying A-level Psychology the examinations are all taken at the end of your 2-year course and the exams include synoptic questions to allow you to demonstrate your ability to draw together your skill, knowledge and understanding from across the full course and to provide extended responses. If you are studying AS Psychology the examinations are taken at the end of your 1-year course.

A-level Paper 1

The topics social influence, memory, attachment and psychopathology are assessed in a written 2-hour exam in which 96 marks are awarded, comprising 33.3% of the A-level. There are four sections in the exam: sections A, B, C, and D, each comprising multiple-choice, short answer and extended writing questions, and in each section 24 marks are awarded.

AS Paper 1

The topics social influence, memory, and attachment are assessed on AS Paper 1 (psychopathology is assessed on AS Paper 2) in a written 1½ hour exam in which 72 marks are awarded, comprising 50% of the AS. There are three sections in the exam: sections A, B, and C, each comprising multiple-choice, short answer and extended writing questions, and in each section 24 marks are awarded.

Assessment objectives: AO1, AO2 and AO3 skills

Assessment objectives (AOs) are set by Ofqual and are the same across all A-level Psychology specifications and all exam boards. The exams measure how you have achieved the assessment objectives outlined in the table below.

AO1	Demonstrate knowledge and understanding of scientific ideas, processes, techniques and procedures.
AO2	Apply knowledge and understanding of scientific ideas, processes, techniques and procedures in a theoretical context; in a practical context; when handling qualitative data and quantitative data.
AO3	Analyse, interpret and evaluate scientific information, ideas and evidence, including in relation to issues, to make judgements and reach conclusions and to develop and refine practical design and procedures

AO1 questions

Identify and **outline** two techniques that may be used in a cognitive interview. (4 marks)

AO2 questions

Evaluate learning theory as an explanation of attachment. (4 marks)

AO1 + AO2 questions

Describe and **evaluate** any two studies of social influence. (12 marks)

AO1 + AO2 + AO3 questions

Outline and **evaluate** research into the effect of leading questions on the accuracy of eyewitness testimony. (8 marks)

Multiple-choice questions

On both A-level and AS papers there are multiple-choice questions and you need to read these carefully. It is important not to jump to conclusions about an answer because one of the options may be a 'distractor'. For multiple-choice questions there will be four or five suggested answers, and usually you will be asked to shade in the 'box' applicable to the answer you suggest. For example:

Which **one** of the following statements is false?

A   Milgram studied obedience.

B   Milgram studied social influence.

C   Milgram studied conformity.

D   Milgram studied minority influence.

Examples of multiple-choice questions are included for each of the four topics. Answers are provided, with some commentary, on pages 87–88.

Effective examination performance

Read the question carefully because marks are awarded only for the specific requirements of the question *as it is set*. Do not waste valuable time answering a question that you wish had been set.

Make a brief plan before you start writing an extended answer. There is space on the exam paper for planning. A plan can be as simple as a list of points, but you must know what, and how much, you plan to write. Time management in exams is vital.

Sometimes a question asks you to outline something. You should practise doing this in order to develop the skill of précis. Be aware of the difference between AO1, AO2 and AO3 commands (injunctions). You will lose marks if you treat AO2 commands such as **evaluate** as an opportunity to write more descriptive (AO1) content. Read the question command carefully and note the relevant skill requirement in your question plan (e.g. outline = AO1, describe = AO1, explain = AO2, evaluate = AO2/AO3).

Marks are awarded **in bands** for:

- AO1: the amount of relevant material presented. Low marks are awarded for brief or inappropriate material and high marks for accurate and detailed material.
- AO2: the level and effectiveness of critical commentary. Low marks are awarded for superficial consideration of a restricted range of issues and high marks for a good range of ideas and specialist terms, and effective use of material addressing a broad range of issues.
- AO3: the extent to which the answer demonstrates a thorough understanding of methods by which psychologists conduct research, for analysis, interpretation, explanation and evaluation of research methodologies and investigative activities.

Question 1 Social influence (1)

Multiple-choice questions

1.1 Which of the following terms best match the statements below? Choose one
term that matches each statement. (5 marks)

    A Internalisation

    B Identification

    C Compliance

    D Majority influence

    E Normative social influence

    This occurs when an individual conforms because he or she believes
that a group norm for behaviour or a group attitude is 'right'.

    This occurs when an individual agrees with the opinions of a group of
people because he or she wishes to be accepted by them.

    This occurs when an individual conforms to a social role but may not
change his or her private opinion.

    This is the process that takes place when an individual's attitudes or
behaviour are affected by the views of the dominant group.

    This occurs when a person conforms to the majority opinion but does
not agree with it.

1.2 Aysha and five of her friends in the cafeteria were deciding whether to go
out clubbing on Saturday night. She didn't really want to go, but all her
friends said they were going, so although she knew she should revise for her
chemistry exam she agreed to go with them.

    Which one of the following terms best explains why Aysha agreed to go? (1 mark)

    A Internalisation

    B Informational social influence

    C Obedience

    D Normative social influence

    E Identification

1.3 Social attitudes have changed a lot in the UK in recent years. For example,
the Church of England has agreed to allow women priests and the law has
been changed to allow same-sex marriage.

    Which one of the following terms best explains these social changes? (1 mark)

    A Normative social influence

    B Informational social influence

    C Minority influence

    D Conversion

    E Majority influence

1.4 Majority influence (conformity) is the process that takes place when an individual's attitudes or behaviour are affected by the views of the dominant group.

When considering social influence, which one of the following statements is **not** true of conformity? (1 mark)

A It occurs between people of equal status

B The emphasis is on social acceptance

C The behaviour is the same as that of the social group

D The motivation for behaviour is explicit

E Participants often deny their behaviour has been influenced by others

1.5 Psychologists have researched why people are able to resist social influence.

When considering resistance to social influence, which one of the following statements is true? (1 mark)

A Males are more able to resist social influence than females

B An authoritarian personality is more able to resist social influence

C A person having an internal locus of control is more able to resist social influence

D A person raised in a collectivist culture is more able to resist social influence

E Older people are more able to resist social influence

Question 2 Social influence (2)

Briefly outline and evaluate the findings of any one study of social influence. (4 marks)

ⓔ Question injunctions are AO1 (outline) and AO3 (evaluate). You need to demonstrate that you know the findings of one study of social influence (e.g. Milgram, Zimbardo, Asch etc.) and can evaluate the findings by referring to methodological issues such as sampling, validity, reliability etc. You should spend about 4 minutes writing.

> **Student A**
>
> Milgram studied obedience to authority and when the context in which the order was given was one of high social status, 26 of the 40 participants (65%) followed orders and administered 450 volt electric shocks. Only 9 of the 40 participants (22.5%) stopped at 315 volts. ⓐ The participants showed signs of extreme tension, they were observed to sweat and tremble and a few laughed nervously. ⓑ One advantage of the Milgram study is that it explains why usually 'good' people may follow immoral orders. ⓒ Another strength is that Milgram collected both objective quantitative findings — the level of electric shock each participant 'stopped' at, as well as qualitative data — how the participants behaved and what they said. The recordings of the verbal comments of the participants show how they refused to take responsibility for the outcomes of their obedient behaviour. ⓓ Also, although the research situation would be unlikely to occur in everyday life the participants clearly believed that the electric shocks were harming Mr Wallace and to this extent the research findings have high ecological validity. ⓔ

ⓔ 4/4 marks awarded. ⓐ, ⓑ Student A provides an accurate and detailed outline of both the quantitative and qualitative findings of the Milgram study. **ⓒ, ⓓ, ⓔ** The evaluation is clear and coherent and the answer is effective because the student explicitly addresses the evaluation points to the *findings* of the research. This is a highly effective answer demonstrating sound knowledge and understanding.

Student B

In the Milgram study 26 of the 40 participants (65%) administered the highest voltage of 450 volt electric shocks. ⓐ The study is unethical as the participants were not told the true purpose of the research and participants were deceived as they thought the electric shocks were real. ⓑ

ⓔ 2/4 marks awarded. ⓐ Student B does not mention social influence or obedience and includes very brief findings. ⓑ This is an accurate evaluation point about the ethics of the study but it is not explicitly related to the findings of the research. This is an ineffective answer.

Question 3 Social influence (3)

Briefly discuss the ethics of research into obedience.   (4 marks)

ⓔ Question injunction = discuss. Because the question is focused on the ethics of research it assesses your AO3 skills. You need to demonstrate your understanding of one or more of the ethical issues arising from research into obedience and why these ethical issues occur. You could discuss problems such as gaining informed consent and/or giving participants the right to withdraw when studying obedience and/or the problems of deciding whether breaking the ethical guidelines can be justified by what we have learned.

Ethical issues arising from the Milgram study include:

- deception and thus prevention of fully informed consent
- psychological harm to the participants caused by the stress of the situation
- the perception of participants that they were unable to withdraw

---

Student A

When studying obedience psychologists should gain fully informed consent from their participants who should be told that their obedience is being studied. Milgram told his participants he was studying memory and learning and the participants were deceived into thinking that the learner, Mr Wallace, was being observed, rather than their obedience. ⓐ Also, participants should not be deceived about what they will be asked to do, but in Milgram participants were deceived, for example, they were led to believe that the electric shocks were real but the learner was only pretending. ⓑ In ethical research, participants are given the right to withdraw, ⓒ but in Milgram's study of obedience participants were prodded to remain even though they were trembling with stress. ⓓ However, at the end of the study, Milgram thoroughly debriefed his participants, who said they were happy to have taken part and this research taught us a

---

lot about why ordinary people can be influenced to obey immoral orders. **e** It is difficult to study obedience without breaking the ethical guidelines as had Milgram told his participants the truth about the experiment they may not have volunteered to participate, and, had Milgram given participants the right to withdraw, there would have been no prods and prompts as 'orders' to obey and Milgram would not have gained a valid measure of obedience. **f**

e **4/4 marks awarded.** **a–d** Student A accurately identifies more than one ethical issue arising from the Milgram research into obedience, and through effective use of material elaborates the ethical issues. **e–f** The student demonstrates sound knowledge and understanding, by providing an argument to defend the research (the debriefing of participants) and an explanation of the value of the research. The strength of this answer is that the student uses psychological terminology accurately to demonstrate a sound understanding of the ethical issues arising in the study of obedience. This is an effective answer.

Student B

Psychologists are supposed to gain fully informed consent from their participants and this means that participants should not be deceived about what they will be asked to do. **a** Milgram broke this ethical guideline because participants were deceived. They were told that the learner was another participant but he was a stooge, and they were led to believe that the electric shocks were real but the learner was only pretending. **b**

e **2/4 marks awarded.** **a**, **b** Student B has identified an appropriate ethical issue arising from the Milgram research but has not even mentioned 'obedience'. The answer is more descriptive than explanatory. This is a common error. To improve this answer the student could have explained the problems involved in the study of obedience, such as the problem of giving the right to withdraw, and/or how to assess the value of research against the right of participants.

Question 4 Social influence (4)

Describe and evaluate research into social influence.   (12 marks)

e Question injunction = describe and evaluate. This question assesses AO1, AO2 and AO3 skills.

For the 'describe' (AO1) part of the question, you should briefly describe research into social influence. There is a wide range of studies that can be included, such as:

■ Asch: research into normative social influence
■ Sherif: research into informational social influence
■ Milgram: study of obedience
■ Zimbardo: study into conformity to social roles
■ Hofling: study of obedience

For the 'evaluate' (AO2/AO3) part of the question, you might focus on the strengths and weaknesses of the methods used in the research you have outlined, and/or evaluate the findings and implications. For high marks you need to express your ideas clearly, using appropriate psychological terminology, to demonstrate a clear understanding. You can address either a broad range of issues in reasonable depth or a narrower range of issues in greater depth. Make sure you focus on the question of research into social influence.

For this split AO1/AO2 question you should write a quick plan before you begin your answer. You need to provide about 6 minutes of content for the AO1 section and 6 minutes of content for the AO2/AO3 section. Do not waste time writing 'all you know about research into social influence' — your answer should provide as much evaluation as content.

Student A

AO1 section

Many psychologists have researched social influence. Sherif aimed to investigate informational social influence and found that the formation of social norms can result when people are asked questions about an ambiguous stimulus. In this study the movement of the spot of light was an illusion but a group norm emerged because individuals looked to others for information. **a** In another study of social influence, Asch conducted a laboratory experiment into normative social influence, and found that student participants gave wrong answers, agreeing with the opinion of the majority of the group, because they wished to be accepted by them. **b**

Zimbardo looked at how social roles have a powerful influence on behaviour. In this study, when young male students were randomly allocated to the role of either prisoner or guard, the allocated role influenced their behaviour. The guards became sadistic and oppressive and the prisoners became passive and depressed. Even when participants were unobserved, they conformed to their roles. **c** Zimbardo concluded that role conformity was due to the social situation rather than to the personal characteristics of the participants, and that social roles have a powerful influence on behaviour. **d**

Hofling studied obedience in a field experiment. Nurses working in a hospital were telephoned by an unknown doctor and asked to administer a drug to a patient. The doctor said he would sign the required paperwork later. To obey, the nurses would have to break hospital rules not to take telephone instructions and not to administer drugs unless the paperwork was completed. Twenty-one nurses obeyed the doctor and would have administered the drug had they not been stopped. The nurses said that they were often given instructions over the telephone and that doctors were annoyed if they refused. **e** In this real-life setting in which doctors have high prestige, legitimate authority and power over nurses, obedience to authority was high. **f**

Questions & Answers

e **6/6 marks awarded.** a–f Student A makes a very effective selection of material in the AO1 section, describing research into social influence. The student provides an accurate and detailed description of a wide range of appropriate research, demonstrating sound knowledge and understanding. The presentation is clear and coherent. a, c, e The strength of this answer is that in the description the student clearly understands what each study tells us about social influence. To save time, the student could have shortened the answer, because most students will struggle to write 300 words in 5–6 minutes.

AO2 section

In the Asch study, because there was a correct answer in the line-matching trials, conformity could be measured in an objective way allowing comparisons to be made. A strength of both Asch and Sherif is that these studies show us how a majority can influence an individual. a However, a weakness of these controlled laboratory experiments is that they do not show how people deal with real world situations that are important, and although the procedures in both these studies have internal validity they lack external realism. Also, both these experiments breach ethical guidelines as the participants did not give informed consent and were deceived. Psychologists should weigh the costs and benefits of unethical research before proceeding. b

Zimbardo showed why people who have power may abuse this, but the artificial situation in this study may have led to demand characteristics where guards and prisoners may have been acting rather than conforming to their roles. c Also in the Zimbardo study, the prisoners and guards were all young and about the same age. A real prison is an established social community in which the prisoners and guards do not all arrive at the same time; so compared to a real prison, the Zimbardo prison situation has low external validity. d

Compared to the Milgram experiment, which was conducted in a specially contrived setting (in a laboratory), the advantage of the Hofling study is that this study was a field experiment carried out in a real hospital setting, giving it high external realism. Also, in Zimbardo and Milgram the all-male participants responded to advertisements and thus they were aware that they were being studied; e but the Hofling sample, all female, were unaware that they were being studied, thus their behaviour was a more valid representation of how they would behave in their everyday lives. f However, the Hofling study only concerns one kind of obedience, because nurses are trained to obey doctors, and thus it cannot be generalised to all other situations. g

---

e **5–6/6 marks awarded.** a–g In the AO2 section the student has identified a broad range of issues and has commented on these issues in reasonable depth and in detail, using appropriate evidence to support the arguments. There is a clear expression of ideas and the student uses a good range of psychological terms. One strength of this answer is that the student uses psychological terminology accurately to demonstrate that he/she has a good understanding of research methods and of the difficulty of drawing any firm conclusions from laboratory studies into social influence. **b**, **d**, **e**, **f** A further strength of this answer is that through effective selection of material it focuses on the question 'as it is set'. Again, most students will struggle to write 300 words of AO2 commentary in 5–6 minutes, but this student has got the balance of AO1/AO2 right, which is important in this type of question. This is an effective answer.

Student B

AO1 section

Asch did a laboratory experiment to study conformity. Students were shown a stimulus line and then three other lines. There was only one 'real' participant in each group. All the participants were asked to say out loud which of the three lines matched the stimulus line. The real participant always answered last or last but one and gave incorrect answers that conformed to the majority view 37% of the time, and 75% conformed at least once. After the experiment, the real participants were asked why they answered as they had and some said they had not wanted to look different. **a**

Zimbardo set up a mock prison to see how the situation influenced behaviour. The prison cells had bars like real prisons and the guards wore military-style uniforms and carried sticks. Male students were allocated to the role of either prisoner or guard. The guards became sadistic and oppressive and their punishments included solitary confinement and humiliation. The prisoners became passive and depressed. Zimbardo concluded that the behaviour was due to the situation rather than to the personal characteristics of the participants. **b**

🅔 2–3/6 marks awarded. Student B gives a basic description that demonstrates some relevant knowledge and understanding. **a**, **b** There is some evidence of selection of material to address the question but, although the basic description of both Asch and Zimbardo is accurate, the student does not elaborate in any explicit detail on what the findings/conclusions tell us about social influence.

AO2 section

The advantage of using a laboratory experiment is that there is control over variables so statements can be made about cause and effect. **a** But the biased sample of male students may not be representative of other populations. **b** Also the Asch study was unethical because he deceived the participants. **c**

The strength of the Zimbardo research is that it is useful, as it can be applied to improve the situation in real prisons, by training guards to treat prisoners differently. **d** The weakness is that the guards and prisoners may have been acting. Also, the participants were all young students so the findings can't be generalised to a real prison. **e**

🅔 2/6 marks awarded. **a–e** In the AO2 section the student provides only a basic commentary and superficial consideration of a restricted range of issues. Some specialist terms are used but the issues are not elaborated or fully explained. The student attempts to evaluate the quoted research and identifies issues but does not explain the extent to which the research does or does not explain the processes of social influence.

NB: Both the example answers first describe evidence and then evaluate the evidence, but you do not have to take this approach. An equally effective approach would be to describe and then evaluate evidence on a 'case by case' basis.

Question 5 Memory (1)

Multiple-choice questions

5.1 According to psychologists we have both short-term and long-term memory. Which one of the following statements is **not** true of short-term memory? (1 mark)

A Limited capacity

B Semantic coding

C Limited duration

D Extended by chunking

E Maintained by rehearsal

5.2 Pablo, who is a concert pianist, is practising the Brahms concerto he will play on Saturday. Which one of the types of memory listed below holds his memories for how to play the piano? (1 mark)

A Semantic memory

B Short-term memory

C Episodic memory

D Procedural memory

E Acoustic memory

5.3 Students are expected to learn and remember a lot of information but often, in an examination, they can't remember what they have learned. Psychologists suggest several reasons why we forget information and one reason for forgetting is **retrieval failure**. Which one of the statements below best explains forgetting due to retrieval failure? (1 mark)

A The memory has disappeared

B New information has replaced the memory of previous information

C The memory cannot be accessed because the context is not similar to when the memory was created

D The central executive of the working memory is overloaded

E The memory has been repressed into the unconscious

5.4 Cosmo and Candy were given 2 minutes to learn a list of 21 words and then 1 minute in which to write down all the words they could remember. The words were: angel, angle, abrupt, chasm, choir, choice, diamond, diminish, demand, famish, fiendish, friendly, horrid, handsome, huddle, joker, jacket, justice, mission, mansion, muddle.

When they were tested Cosmo remembered 7 words and Candy remembered 8 words. Which one of the following statements best explains why they remembered so few of the words? (1 mark)

A   Interference from earlier memories

B   Limited capacity of short-term memory

C   Retrieval failure

D   Rehearsal failure

E   Central executive overload

5.5 Psychologists have researched factors that influence the accuracy of eyewitness testimony. Which of the factors listed below has been found to create a false memory?   (1 mark)

A   The witness had poor eyesight

B   The witness was interviewed using a standard interview technique

C   The witness was asked a leading question

D   The witness was interviewed more than once

E   The witness was anxious and stressed

Question 6 Memory (2)

Briefly describe the working memory model.   (4 marks)

ⓔ Question injunction = briefly describe. This question requires you to show AO1 skills. You need to demonstrate your understanding of the key features of the working memory model by giving a brief description of the components of the model and of their functions. You are not required to give evidence that supports the model or the strengths and limitations of the model. You are not expected to provide more than 4 minutes of writing.

Student A

The working memory model proposes that STM is an active processor in which the central executive 'attends to and works on' either speech-based information or visually coded information. **a** The central executive processes information from all sensory routes; this process is 'attention-like', having limited capacity. **b** The articulatory–phonological loop processes speech-based information. The phonological store focuses on incoming speech perception and the articulatory process focuses on speech production. **c** The visuospatial working area is where spatial and visual information is processed. **d**

ⓔ **4/4 marks awarded. a–d** The student provides an accurate and detailed description of the working memory model that demonstrates a sound understanding of all three components of the model and of their function.

Student B

The working memory model is a model of STM having three parts. The central executive. **a** The phonological loop processes speech-based information. The visuospatial working area processes visual information.

ⓔ **2/4 marks awarded.** This answer provides a basic outline of the working memory model, shows some understanding that the working memory model is a model of STM and gives an accurate but basic outline of the three component parts. The weakness of this answer is that it is like a list and **a** gives no information about the function of the central executive.

Question 7 Memory (3)

Describe the multi-store model of memory.   (4 marks)

ⓔ Question injunction = describe. This question requires you to show AO1 skills. You need to demonstrate your understanding of the multi-store model of memory by writing a detailed and accurate description. You are not required to give evidence that supports the model or the strengths and limitations of the model. You are not expected to provide more than 4 minutes of writing. To describe the model, you should identify the components of the model and their function.

> **Student A**
>
> The multi-store model suggests that memory consists of different stores, sensory memory, short-term memory (STM) and long-term memory (LTM). **a** Sensory memory is where information enters the system through our senses (e.g. our eyes and ears). If the information in sensory memory is attended to, it will be passed to the STM store which has limited capacity for about seven chunks of information. **b** Verbal rehearsal maintains information in STM, but STM has limited duration, thus the information may be lost if it is displaced by new incoming information. **c** Information is passed from STM to LTM by rehearsing the information and LTM has unlimited capacity and duration so the information may be remembered for a lifetime. **d**

ⓔ **4/4 marks awarded.** **a–d** Student A provides a thorough, accurate and detailed description of the multi-store model of memory, which demonstrates a sound understanding of all three components of the model, of their function, of the characteristics of STM and LTM, and of the differences between STM and LTM.

> **Student B**
>
> The multi-store model proposes that memory consists of different stores, sensory memory, short-term memory (STM) and long-term memory (LTM). Information is passed from STM to LTM by rehearsing information. **a** Like when we repeat a telephone number so we don't forget it.

ⓔ **2/4 marks awarded.** Student B provides a basic description of the multi-store model and gives an accurate but very brief outline of the three memory stores. **a** Credit would be given for the accurate suggestion that information is passed from STM to LTM by rehearsal. The weakness of the answer is that it gives no information about the functions of the three memory stores or the differences between them.

Question 8 Memory (4)

Describe and evaluate research into the effect of leading questions on the accuracy of eyewitness testimony.

(16 marks)

ⓔ Question injunction = describe and evaluate. This question assesses AO1, AO2 and AO3 skills.

For the 'describe' (AO1) part of the question, you should briefly describe research into the effect of leading questions on eyewitness testimony. You could include:

- Loftus and Palmer
- Yuille and Cutshall

For the 'evaluate' (AO2/AO3) part of the question, you might focus on the strengths and weaknesses of the methods used in the research, and/or evaluate the findings and implications. For high marks you need to express your ideas clearly, using appropriate psychological terminology, to demonstrate a solid understanding. You can address either a broad range of issues in reasonable depth or a narrower range of issues in greater depth. Make sure you focus on the question of the effect of leading questions on eyewitness testimony.

For this question you should write a quick plan before you begin your answer. You need to provide about 7 minutes of content for the AO1 section and 7 minutes of critical argument for the AO2/AO3 section and your answer should include as much evaluation as content.

In the evaluation section, possible answers could include:

- the extent to which research has internal (experimental) validity
- the laboratory environment in which much research into EWT is undertaken
- participants not being as emotionally aroused or feeling the same sense of responsibility as they would in a real incident
- the lack of realism in tasks when participants watch video films as compared to observing a real event
- how representative the samples used in research are
- the usefulness of research

You need to write an explanation that demonstrates your understanding of the advantages and disadvantages of the research methodologies used.

Student answer

AO1 section

Loftus and Palmer conducted a laboratory experiment looking at the effect of leading questions on eyewitness memory. In the first experiment, 45 student participants all watched a video of a car crash. After writing a description of the crash they had seen, they were divided into five groups and asked to complete a questionnaire in which they were asked to estimate the speed the cars were travelling when they 'contacted, bumped, collided, hit or smashed'. These five different words were the independent variable and Loftus and Palmer hypothesised that the students who were asked the leading question using the word 'smashed' would estimate the highest speed. **a** In a follow-up experiment, Loftus and Palmer asked 150 students to watch a video of a multiple car crash. After writing a description of what they had seen they were divided into three groups of 50 and asked to complete a questionnaire. Group 1 were asked to estimate the speed the cars were travelling when they 'hit' each other, group 2 were asked to estimate the speed the cars were travelling when they 'smashed into' each other, and group 3, the control group, were not asked a question about the speed of the cars. A week later, all 150 students were asked whether they saw any broken glass in the video — there was no broken glass in the film. The group who had been asked a question using the word 'smashed' were significantly more likely to report seeing broken glass than either the 'hit' group or the control group. **b** Loftus and Palmer concluded that the false memory of seeing broken glass had been created by asking the leading question using the word 'smashed' because 'smashed' implies breakage, and thus 'breakage' was added to the memory of the car crash. **c** This research demonstrates that leading questions reduce the accuracy of eyewitness testimony. **d**

e In the AO1 section, student A provides an accurate and detailed description of the Loftus and Palmer research into eyewitness testimony. **a**, **b** One strength of this answer is that the student accurately describes both the samples, methods, procedures and findings of experiment 1 and experiment 2. **c**, **d** A further strength of the answer is that the conclusions of this research are described accurately. The answer demonstrates understanding of how the false memory was created, and then explicitly relates the findings of this research to the question of accuracy of eyewitness memory.

AO2/AO3 section

One of the advantages of using laboratory experiments to research the effect of leading questions is that standardised procedures and high levels of control increase both validity and reliability. **a** Validity is increased because other variables that could affect what is being measured are controlled. **b** In Loftus and Palmer all the participants watched the same video in the same environment, and except for the word used in the leading question, all were asked the same questions. Additionally, in the second experiment, the control group was not asked a leading question, so internal validity was high as the changed wording of the question must have been the only cause of the differing speed estimates and the false memories of seeing broken glass. **c**

However, ecological validity (external validity) refers to the extent to which the procedures used in research are realistic in that they could happen in real life, and the extent to which the sample of participants is representative of the type of people who might be eyewitnesses to a real incident. **d** Much of the research into EWT has been laboratory experiments (e.g. the Loftus and Palmer research). This research can be criticised as having low ecological validity, because when watching a video film, participants will not be as emotionally aroused as they would be in a real incident (no surprise or danger) and they will not feel the same sense of responsibility when they answer questions about what they have witnessed. e Also, as in the Loftus and Palmer research, much research into eyewitness testimony involves laboratory experiments using student samples. This reduces the ecological validity because students spend much of their time memorising information, which would not be the case with witnesses to a real incident. f

e **13–14/16 marks awarded.** a, b In the AO2/AO3 section, student A begins by demonstrating sound understanding of the advantages of experimental research. c The student then goes on to accurately apply this understanding to the Loftus and Palmer research. d, e, f The answer gives an accurate definition of ecological validity followed by a quite detailed explanation for why the Loftus and Palmer research may lack ecological validity.

The strength of this answer is that the student has focused on the question, used accurate and appropriate terminology, demonstrating knowledge and understanding. The answer could have been improved by contrasting the Loftus and Palmer findings with the findings of non-laboratory research, or perhaps by remarking on the usefulness of the research. Overall, this answer is clear and focused, the knowledge of research is accurate and detailed and the evaluation is thorough and effective.

Student B

AO1 section

Loftus and Palmer wanted to find out whether leading questions affect eyewitness memory: 45 participants all watched a video of a car crash and were then divided into five groups to complete a questionnaire. On the questionnaire they were asked to estimate the speed the cars were travelling when they 'contacted, bumped, collided, hit or smashed'. The students who were asked the question using the word 'smashed' estimated the highest speed at 9 mph faster than the lowest speed. a Loftus and Palmer concluded that the increased speed estimate was caused by the way the question was asked because 'smashed' implies a harder crash than 'bumped' or 'collided'. This research shows that leading questions affect memory. b

e a In the AO1 section, the description of the research is very brief and although accurate only outlines the sample, procedure and findings of the first Loftus and Palmer experiment. b The student then makes a final statement about the effect of leading questions on memory that is not explained.

AO2/AO3 section

This research had a high level of validity because all the participants watched the same video in the same environment, and except for the word used in the leading question, all were asked the same questions. a

However, ecological validity is low because when watching a video film, participants will not be as emotionally aroused as they would be in a real

> incident. **b** Also a 2D film does not contain the same cues to speed as a 3D event so students might have found it difficult to estimate speed. **c** Also, all the participants were students who are mostly young adults and real witnesses will be of a wider age range. **d** Overall we can't be certain that leading questions would have the same effect on the memories of a real eyewitness. **e**

e **7–8/16 marks awarded.** **a** In the AO2/AO3 section, the point about validity, though accurate, is not fully explained. **b**, **c**, **d** The points about ecological validity are stronger and quite thorough but, though explained, these points read rather like a list. **e** The final sentence is accurate but not explicitly related to the question of eyewitness testimony. The weakness of the answer is that it reads as an evaluation of the Loftus and Palmer research rather than as an answer to the question as set.

This answer could have been strengthened by increasing the amount of detail in the descriptive section, by adding explanation and argument to the evaluation section, and by relating evaluative points to the question of eyewitness testimony. Overall, although knowledge of research is present the evaluation is only partially effective and the answer lacks organisation and focus.

Question 9 Attachment (1)

Multiple-choice questions

9.1 Schaffer and Emerson (1964) studied babies at monthly intervals for the first 18 months of life. The babies were visited monthly for approximately 1 year, their interactions with their caregivers were observed, and caregivers were interviewed. They discovered that a baby's attachments develop in a specific sequence.

Which one of the following statements is not one of the stages of development of attachment? (1 mark)

A Indiscriminate attachments where babies respond equally to any caregiver

B Preference for certain people where babies distinguish primary and secondary caregivers but accept care from anyone

C Preference for a single attachment figure where the baby shows fear of strangers and unhappiness when separated from a special person

D Secure attachments where the baby shows some anxiety when their caregiver departs but are easily soothed and greet the caregiver's return with enthusiasm

E Multiple attachments where the baby forms several attachments

9.2 Psychologists have found that several factors influence the development of attachments.

Which **three** of the following list of factors influence the development of attachment? (3 marks)

A The age of the child

B Intelligence of parents

C The child's temperament

D Attending a day nursery

E The quality of care

9.3 In cross-cultural research, van Ijzendoorn and Kroonenberg (1988) studied attachment styles of infants in eight different countries.

Which one of the following list of countries was not included in this research? (1 mark)

A Great Britain

B Japan

C Sweden

D France

E USA

9.4 Louis has just started attending day nursery. In the morning when his mother leaves him at nursery he doesn't seem to mind, he tends to play on his own, and when his mother collects him he doesn't run to be picked up or want to hold her hand.

Which one of the following terms best describes Louis's attachment style? (1 mark)

A Secure attachment

B Insecure–avoidant attachment

C Insecure–resistant attachment

9.5 Hodges and Tizard (1989) looked at whether there is a critical period in which failure to make a secure attachment can be shown to affect adult relationships. They studied a group of children from their early days in an institution until they were 16 years old.

Which one of the statements below best describes the children's experience while they were in the institution? (1 mark)

A Failure of attachment

B Maternal privation

C Separation from attachment figure

D Maternal deprivation

E Maternal neglect

Question 10 Attachment (2)

Outline and evaluate learning theory as an explanation of attachment formation. (8 marks)

ⓔ Question injunction = outline and evaluate. This question requires you to show AO1 and AO2 skills. You need to demonstrate your understanding of the features of learning theory as an explanation of attachment. Your outline should demonstrate that you understand the behaviourist perspective.

Your AO1 outline could focus on the following:

- Attachment is learned through conditioning.
- Attachment bonds are developed because of the association between the pleasure of receiving food and the person who is feeding the infant.
- Attachment bonds are developed because of operant conditioning — positive reinforcement because being close to the caregiver gives pleasure.

Your AO2 evaluation could focus on the following:

- Operant conditioning — reinforcement by the provision of food — cannot fully explain attachment.
- It is reductionist as it ignores factors other than reinforcement that influence attachment.
- It cannot explain why there are different types of attachment.

Student A

AO1 section

The learning explanation proposes that a child's attachment bond with his or her caregiver can be explained in terms of operant conditioning. **a** Based on operant conditioning, infants feel discomfort when they are hungry and so desire food to remove the discomfort. **b** They learn that if they cry, their caregiver feeds them and the discomfort is removed. **c** This is negative reinforcement: the consequences of behaviour (crying) lead to something unpleasant ceasing (feeling hungry stops). **d** Thus, the behaviour of 'being close' to the caregiver is reinforced, the attachment bond is learned and the attachment behaviour of distress is shown if the child is separated from the caregiver. **e**

---

e Student A provides an accurate and detailed outline of the learning theory of the development of attachments. **a–e** The answer demonstrates a sound understanding of the key features of learning theory and how this can be applied to explain the development of attachment. The strength of this answer is in the accurate use of psychological terminology.

AO2 section

However, learning theory, or operant conditioning as a result of the provision of food, cannot fully explain the development of attachment. In a study of monkeys, Harlow demonstrated that even though the wire mother provided food the baby monkeys did not become attached to it, preferring to cling to the cloth covered monkey for comfort — which suggests that factors other than the provision of food as a reward are important. **a** Also, learning theory is reductionist as it reduces complex human behaviour to a simplistic explanation. **b** Factors other than reinforcement and learning have been found to influence the development of attachment. Bowlby proposed that unless attachments have developed by between 1 and 3 years, they do not develop normally and if learning is the only explanation for attachment this would not be the case. **c** Also, learning theory focuses on nurture and ignores factors such as the child's innate temperament which may make it easier or harder to form attachments. **d** Another factor that learning theory tends to ignore is the quality of the care provided and Ainsworth suggests that sensitivity of the caregiver can also affect the development of attachments. **e** Finally, there are individual differences in the type of attachment developed which would not be the case if attachment bonds were learned only as a result of feeding/reinforcement. **f**

e **8/8 marks awarded.** The evaluation section is effective, clear, coherent and focused. Specialist terminology is used accurately. **a** The student supports the point made by referring to research and explaining what this means for learning theory. **b** The point about reductionism is accurately defined. **c**, **d**, **e**, **f** The student criticises learning theory by making a wide range of accurate points clearly and concisely.

Student B

AO1 section

Learning theory proposes that a child's attachment bond with his or her caregiver, can be explained in terms of operant conditioning — the reinforcement (pleasure) arising from the satisfaction of basic needs such as food and drink. The mother (or caregiver) provides pleasure and the infant learns to associate pleasure with the caregiver. **a**

e Student B provides a basic description of the learning theory of the development of attachment. **a** Credit would be given for the fairly brief, but accurate, description of how operant conditioning may explain the development of the attachment bond. The weakness of this answer is that, although accurate, it is very brief.

AO2 section

However, learning theory is reductionist as it only looks at nurture not nature. **a** Factors such as the child's innate temperament are ignored which may make it easier or harder to form attachments. **b** Ainsworth suggests that sensitivity of the caregiver can also affect the development of attachments. **c** Also, there are individual differences in attachments, secure and insecure, which cannot be explained by operant conditioning. **d**

e **4–5/8 marks.** This evaluation is brief and could be argued more effectively. **a** The point about reductionism is not effectively argued. **b**, **c** These points are stated rather than explained. **d** This point is accurate but could be argued more effectively and related to learning theory. Overall, knowledge is evident, there is some effective evaluation, and specialist terminology is mostly used accurately.

Question 11 Attachment (3)

Compare Bowlby's explanation of attachment with the learning theory of attachment.

(4 marks)

ⓔ Question injunction = compare. This question requires you to show AO2 skills. You need to demonstrate your understanding by writing a brief but accurate explanation of the difference between Bowlby's theory and the learning explanations of attachment. The question does not require you to describe the explanations. To gain high marks you need to explain the consequences or implications of the differences you suggest. Possible differences include the following:

■ According to Bowlby, infants are innately programmed to form attachment, so attachment is biological rather than learned.
■ The learning theory suggests no critical period — attachments can be learned and relearned.
■ The learning theory does not suggest that attachment is the basis, or template, for future relationships and thus does not predict negative long-term consequences following disruption of attachment.

You are not expected to provide more than about 4 minutes of writing. In your answer you should first identify one or more differences and then explain the implications of the difference(s).

Student A

The main difference between Bowlby's and the learning (behaviourist) explanation is that Bowlby suggests that infants are biologically programmed to develop attachments and thus that attachments form because of innate biological characteristics while learning theory suggests that attachments develop because of nurture (learning from experience). **a** Bowlby also suggests that there may be a critical period in which attachment bonds may develop but behavioural theorists suggest that attachment bonds should be able to be learned (and relearned) at any age. **b** A final difference is that, unlike Bowlby, learning theory does not suggest that attachment creates a schema for future relationships. **c**

ⓔ **4/4 marks awarded.** Student A provides an accurate and detailed comparison, demonstrating an understanding of the difference between the theories, and of the implications of these differences. **a, b, c** Although the student focuses on differences, the strength of the answer is that the student uses psychological terminology accurately to demonstrate an accurate understanding of the key features of both Bowlby's and the learning explanation.

Student B

Bowlby suggests that infants are biologically programmed to form attachments and thus that attachments are innate (nature) while learning theory says attachments develop because of nurture. **a**

 1–2/4 marks awarded. a Student B outlines a feature of Bowlby's explanation — but while the answer is accurate, it is little more than a statement and only the final part of the sentence touches on a difference between the two explanations. The weakness of this answer is that the student has not elaborated and explained the difference identified.

Question 12 Attachment (4)

Explain ethical problems associated with an observational study of children. (4 marks)

 Question injunction = explain. Because this question relates to research methods, this assesses your AO3 skills. You need to demonstrate your understanding of the issues involved in conducting ethical research involving children.

Ethical problems might include:

- informed consent
- failure to protect, in that the absence of the mother causes distress
- confidentiality
- the right to withdraw might bias the sample

Student A

One ethical problem when observing children is that having given their informed consent the parent must be allowed the right to withdraw the child from the research, a and if they choose to withdraw their child, this may result in a biased sample of participants. b Another ethical issue is protecting the children from harm or distress which means that when observing young children they should not be separated from their caregivers. c

 4/4 marks awarded. a–c Student A identifies and explains more than one appropriate ethical issue and clearly demonstrates understanding of ethical research. The strength of this answer is that the student uses psychological terminology accurately to demonstrate that he or she has a good understanding of the ethical problems that can arise when involving young children in observational research.

Student B

An ethical problem when observing children is that parents must be asked to give informed consent, but they might not want to which means that obtaining a sample may be difficult.

 2/4 marks awarded. Student B identifies an appropriate ethical issue and briefly explains its implications, but the weakness of the answer is that the student only identifies one ethical problem and the question asked for 'ethical problems'.

Question 13 Psychopathology (1)

NB: Psychopathology is examined on AS Paper 2.

Multiple-choice questions

13.1 Several conditions are associated with ideal mental health. Which **four** of the following statements match these conditions? (4 marks)

  A Having a positive self-attitude and high self-esteem

  B Being motivated to realise personal growth

  C Having the ability to cope with stress

  D Having supportive friends

  E Having an accurate perception of reality

13.2 Maddie never goes into her house with shoes on, she cleans the floors over and over again, and she worries about germs getting onto the floor from dirty feet. Recently she has stopped going out much as she worries that if she goes out her feet will be contaminated. She feels anxious and miserable.

Which one of the following disorders best matches Maddie's problem? (1 mark)

  A Depression

  B OCD

  C Agoraphobia

  D Phobia

13.3 The behaviourist approach makes several assumptions about the causes of abnormal behaviour. Which **three** of the following statements match these assumptions? (3 marks)

  A Abnormal behaviour is nature not nurture

  B Abnormal behaviour is learned

  C Abnormal behaviour is learned by association

  D Abnormal behaviour may be genetic

  E Abnormal behaviour is not a symptom of some underlying cause

13.4 A researcher wanted to find out whether chickens could learn. She put a chicken in a box from which it could escape by pecking a blue peg. Each time the chicken escaped it was given corn as a food treat. At first the chicken took a long time to escape but after 10 trials the chicken could escape immediately.

Which one of the following types of learning is being studied in this experiment? (1 mark)

  A Classical conditioning

  B Observational learning

  C Systematic desensitisation

  D Positive reinforcement

  E Operant conditioning

13.5 Beck's negative triad can be used to explain depression. Which **three** of the statements below best describe this cognitive triad? (3 marks)

    A   Negative views about the self

    B   Negative views about the family

    C   Negative views about the future

    D   Negative views about my job

    E   Negative views about the world

Question 14 Psychopathology (2)

NB: Psychopathology is examined on AS Paper 2.

Explain how systematic desensitisation may be used to treat a phobia of flying. (4 marks)

ⓔ Question injunction = explain. This question assesses AO2 skills, and marks are awarded if you apply your knowledge and understanding to an unfamiliar situation. Your answer should include:

- a brief explanation of the process of systematic desensitisation
- an identification of elements in the hierarchy of fears
- how clients learn to associate pleasant relaxation with fear-provoking situations
- the step-by-step approach through the hierarchy of fears

Your answer must be explanatory rather than descriptive and you are not expected to provide more than 4 minutes of writing.

> **Student A**
>
> Based on the behaviourist approach, systematic desensitisation is based on learning to associate a feared stimulus with a pleasant response. a During systematic desensitisation the phobia is broken down into the small stimulus–response units that comprise it and these units are ranked into a hierarchy from the least worrying to the most fearful situation. In a fear of flying the least fearful situation might be thinking about air travel when planning a holiday and the most feared situation might be boarding a plane. b During therapy, the therapist first teaches the client to enjoy relaxation c and then works though each stimulus–response unit in the hierarchy, from the least feared stimulus to the most feared stimulus, helping the person to replace each unwanted response of being afraid by the pleasure of feeling relaxed. d If the therapy is successful, eventually the fear of flying will be eliminated.

ⓔ **4/4 marks awarded.** Student A has given an effective and accurate explanation of the process of systematic desensitisation and has applied this to a fear of flying. a–d The strengths of this answer are that the student has, using appropriate terminology, explained the process of systematic desensitisation and has given an appropriate example of a possible hierarchy of fears of flying.

Systematic desensitisation helps people to gradually learn to associate a feared stimulus with a pleasant response such as relaxation, so the person with the phobia works with a therapist to learn to relax and eventually the fear will be cured.

(e) **1/4 marks awarded.** Student B has given a basic outline which demonstrates some relevant knowledge and understanding, but the answer should be more detailed and much more clearly applied to a fear of flying.

Question 15 Psychopathology (3)

NB: Psychopathology is examined on AS Paper 2.

Discuss the extent to which drug treatment is an effective way to treat OCD.   (12 marks)

(e) Question injunction = discuss. This question assesses AO2 skills, and marks are awarded if you apply your knowledge and understanding of the appropriateness of drug treatment for OCD.

Your answer could include commentary on:

- the advantage of drug therapies that drug treatment can quickly relieve conditions such as OCD so that people are able to lead normal lives
- the advantage of drug treatment that it may allow a patient to be well enough to receive psychological treatment
- the disadvantage of drug treatment that drugs may result in addiction or may cause unwanted side effects
- the disadvantage of drug treatment that drugs may hide the cause of the problem, which may re-occur when the patient stops taking the drug
- drug treatment being based on the assumption that OCD has an underlying biological cause
- the reductionist approach, because drug therapies ignore possible psychosocial factors involved in abnormal behaviour
- the ethical problems that arise when drug therapy is used to control behaviour that we do not understand

Your answer must be evaluative rather than descriptive and you are not expected to provide more than 12 minutes of writing.

It can be argued that if the cause of OCD is known to be biological, then drug treatment is appropriate. Research looking at the human serotonin transporter gene found that six out of seven people in two separate families who had one gene mutation had OCD and the four people with the most severe OCD symptoms had a second mutation in the same gene. This suggests a biological cause for OCD and that the neurotransmitter serotonin may be involved in causing OCD. If this is the case then drug treatment should be effective because drugs quickly relieve symptoms, enabling patients to manage their lives more easily. a

For example, selective serotonin reuptake inhibitor (SSRI) drugs such as Prozac, that increase levels of the neurotransmitter serotonin, have been found to be an effective treatment for anxiety disorders such as OCD. **b** Another reason why drug treatment may be effective is that taking anti-anxiety drugs only requires the patient to remember to take the drugs, and does not involve changes of lifestyle. **c** However, unless there is a clearly understood biological cause for the problem, drug treatment may not be effective because drugs may only provide temporary relief from symptoms, and when the patient stops taking the drugs the symptoms of OCD may recur. **d** A further problem is that it may be difficult to separate the effect of the drug from any placebo effect, so it may be difficult to gain a valid measure of the effectiveness of treatment. **e** That said, an advantage of drug treatment is that drugs can be used either to prepare people for, or together with, psychological therapy such as CBT. **f** Finally, ethical issues may arise because, if we do not know what effect a drug will have, it will be difficult to obtain fully informed consent to the treatment, and as each patient with OCD will have different obsessions and compulsions, patients may respond differently to the same drug treatment and treating drug-induced side effects can be problematic. **g**

e **11/12 marks awarded.** Student A has written a strong answer. **a–g** The material is used effectively and a broad range of issues are evaluated in some depth. The student expresses ideas clearly using a range of specialist terms accurately to demonstrate relevant and sound knowledge and understanding. **a** One strength of the answer is the use of evidence to support the argument about the effectiveness of drug treatment and the demonstration of knowledge of drug treatment for treating OCD is accurate and detailed. Evaluation is effective. Overall, the answer is clear, coherent and focused on treating OCD.

Student B

Drug treatment is effective because it quickly relieves symptoms and enables people with OCD to live near-normal lives. **a** Also, drug treatment is effective because taking drugs only requires the patient to remember to take the drugs, and does not involve changes of lifestyle. **b** However, drugs cause side effects and may only provide temporary relief from symptoms, so when the patient stops taking the drugs the symptoms may recur. **c** An advantage is that drug treatment can be used with psychological therapy. However, there may be individual differences in the effectiveness of drugs and in the quantity of side effects. **d**

e **4–5/12 marks awarded.** Student B has provided a reasonable commentary, although the material is not always used effectively. **a–d** A range of issues related to drug treatment is evaluated in limited depth but not explicitly applied to the treatment of OCD. The student expresses ideas using a range of specialist terms accurately and demonstrates some relevant knowledge and understanding. To improve this answer, the student could have addressed the requirements of the question with more clarity and given examples to illustrate the issues.

Question 16 Psychopathology (4)

NB: Psychopathology is examined on AS Paper 2.

Outline the cognitive approach to explaining depression.   (6 marks)

e Question injunction = outline. This question assesses AO1 skills, and marks are awarded if you demonstrate your understanding of the psychodynamic approach.

You could include:

- the role of the conscious mind as a cause of behaviour
- the theory that irrational thought processes cause depression
- Beck's cognitive triad
- the theory that people can be helped to think more rationally

You are not expected to provide more than 6 minutes of writing.

Student A

The cognitive approach to depression assumes that the human mind is like an information processor and that people are able to control how they select, store and think about information. **a** In the cognitive approach, depression is caused when people have negative thoughts about themselves and the future. Beck found that irrational beliefs were common in patients suffering from depression and depressed people believe that they are unloved and that nothing good will ever happen in the future. **b** Overall, the cognitive approach explains depression in terms of an overly pessimistic outlook on life. Beck describes the 'cognitive triad' in which a depressed patient has a negative view of themselves, the world and the future. The cognitive approach views the negative way of thinking as the cause of depression. **c**

---

e **5/6 marks awarded.** Student A has given an accurate and detailed outline demonstrating relevant knowledge and understanding of the cognitive explanation for depression. **a–c** Beck's cognitive triad is used to address the question. The strength of this answer is that the student has, using appropriate terminology, given a coherent and accurate outline of the cognitive explanation for depression.

Student B

In the cognitive approach, depression is caused by irrational thinking when people have negative thoughts. **a** Beck describes a cognitive triad, in which a depressed patient has a negative view of themselves, the world and the future. **b** The cognitive approach views the irrational way of thinking as the causes of depression and suggests that CBT be used to help people think more rationally. **c**

ⓔ 3–4/6 marks awarded. Student B has given an accurate but basic outline demonstrating some relevant knowledge and understanding, but the answer could be more detailed. **ⓒ** Rather than repeating the first sentence, to improve this answer the student could have given more detail about the cognitive explanation for OCD.

Multiple-choice answers

Social influence

1.1 Correct answers:

A Internalisation. This occurs when an individual conforms because he or she believes that a group norm for behaviour or a group attitude is 'right'.

B Identification. This occurs when an individual conforms to a social role but may not change his or her private opinion.

C Compliance. This occurs when a person conforms to the majority opinion but does not agree with it.

D Majority influence. This is the process that takes place when an individual's attitudes or behaviour are affected by the views of the dominant group.

E Normative social influence. This occurs when an individual agrees with the opinions of a group of people because he or she wishes to be accepted by them.

1.2 The answer is D. Normative social influence occurs when an individual agrees with the opinions of a group of people because he or she wishes to be accepted by them. Aysha wanted to be accepted by her friends so agreed to go clubbing even though privately she knew she should revise.

1.3 The answer is C. Minority influence is the process that takes place when a consistent minority changes the attitudes and/or behaviour of individuals in society. Minority influence leads to a change in attitudes and involves the process of conversion.

1.4 The answer is D. In conformity the motivation to change attitudes or behaviour to fit in with a majority group or social norms is implicit rather than explicit.

1.5 The answer is C. A person having an internal locus of control is more able to resist social influence.

Memory

5.1 The answer is B. According to Baddeley (1966), in short-term memory, memories are acoustically encoded, that is, encoded by sound rather than by meaning.

5.2 The answer is D. Procedural memory is the part of the long-term memory responsible for motor skills as it stores information on how to perform learned behaviours, such as playing the piano. Procedural memories are implicit and do not involve conscious thought.

5.3 The answer is C. Forgetting due to retrieval failure is when information in long-term memory cannot be remembered because the retrieval cues are not present. When we store a memory we store information about the situation known as retrieval cues and these retrieval cues can help trigger the memory. Retrieval cues can be context cues, such as the environment, or internal cues such as our mood or physical state.

5.4 The answer is B. Short-term memory (STM) has a limited capacity of 7–9 items of information. Cosmo and Candy had 21 words to learn in 2 minutes and because of the limited capacity of STM most of the words would have been displaced (pushed out of STM) by the later words.

5.5 The answer is C. Loftus and Palmer found that if an eyewitness is asked a leading question, the meaning of the question may become part of the memory thus changing the memory and causing a false memory.

Attachment

9.1 The answer is D. A secure attachment is a type of attachment rather than a stage of attachment.

9.2 The correct answers are A, C and E. The age of the child: Bowlby proposed that unless attachments have developed by between 1 and 3 years, they will not develop 'normally'. The child's temperament may make it easier or harder for him or her to form attachments. The quality of care and the sensitivity of the caregiver can also affect the development of attachments.

9.3 The answer is D. France was not included. The eight countries were West Germany, Great Britain, Netherlands, Sweden, Israel, Japan, China, USA.

9.4 The answer is B. In **insecure–avoidant attachment** the infant shows indifference when the caregiver leaves and at reunion the infant actively avoids contact with the caregiver. These infants tend to play independently.

9.5 The answer is B. Privation means never having been able to satisfy a certain need. Maternal privation is when a child has never been able to form a close relationship (develop an attachment) with any one caregiver.

Psychopathology

13.1 The correct answers are A, B, C and E. Having supportive friends may be helpful but is not on the list. Being in control and making your own decisions (personal autonomy) and having the ability to adapt to changes in one's environment are the other two conditions.

13.2 The answer is B. Those who suffer from OCD have a persistent fear of a specific object or situation, they recognise their fear is excessive, but exposure to the phobic stimulus, in Maddie's case the thought of dirt on the floor or her feet, produces a rapid anxiety response.

13.3 The correct answers are B, C and E. Behaviourist psychologists do not suggest biological causes for normal or abnormal behaviour.

13.4 The correct answer is E. Operant conditioning means that if we are rewarded for behaviour we are more likely to repeat it. The chicken was rewarded for pecking the blue peg by being given food. Operant conditioning involves positive reinforcement (or negative reinforcement). The food the chicken was given was positive reinforcement, but though reinforcement is involved in the process of learning, it is not a type of learning.

13.5 The correct answers are A, C and E. According to Beck the negative triad comprises negative views about self, the future and the world.

Knowledge check answers

1 Compliance occurs when a person conforms to the majority opinion in public but in private does not agree. Compliance occurs because an individual wishes to be accepted by a majority group.

2 The guards became sadistic and oppressive and increased the length of the line-ups until some of them lasted several hours. They decided that the prisoners should receive their rights only as a privilege, in return for good behaviour. Guards gave out punishments that included solitary confinement and humiliation. The prisoners became passive and depressed. Five prisoners had to be released early because of extreme depression and these symptoms had started to appear within 2 days.

3 Within a social hierarchy, the emphasis is on social power and obedience occurs between people of unequal status, whereas conformity occurs between people of equal status and the emphasis is on social acceptance.

4 Twenty-six of the 40 participants went all the way to 450 volts with electric shocks. The participants shook and trembled, and argued with the experimenter.

5 Some people have an authoritarian personality, characterised by a submissive attitude to authority. These people are more likely to obey a legitimate authority.

6 Locus of control — those having an internal locus of control see themselves as responsible for what happens to them and are more likely to resist pressure to conform or obey authority. People with an advanced level of moral development may resist pressure to obey an immoral order.

7 Moral development, because levels of moral development vary between individuals. Locus of control, because those having an external locus of control may be more likely to obey a legitimate authority.

8 A laboratory experiment.

9 They are consistent and they draw attention to their views. They take action in support of their principles (e.g. take part in protest marches). They are similar, in terms of age, class and gender, to the population they are trying to influence.

10 The capacity for memory is approximately 'seven plus or minus two' pieces of information.

11 STM has limited capacity, approximately seven to nine pieces of information, but LTM has unlimited capacity. Information in STM has limited duration, about 30 seconds, but information in LTM may last a lifetime.

12 The primacy effect occurs because, when a list of information is being memorised, the first items of information are likely to have been transferred to LTM, and the recency effect happens because the last items of information are still in STM.

13 Procedural memory stores information on how to perform certain procedures, such as walking, talking, typing, playing the piano, riding a bike.

Procedural memories are implicit and do not involve conscious thought.

14 One assumption of the working memory model is that the articulatory–phonological loop has limited capacity. The interference task technique involves a participant being asked to perform two tasks that use the articulatory–phonological loop, such as reading a book while singing a song. If their performance on both tasks is affected, this is because the articulatory–phonological loop cannot cope with both tasks.

15 Simeon revised his French vocabulary and after lunch he revised his Spanish vocabulary. French and Spanish are similar languages and revising his Spanish later may have disrupted the memory of his French vocabulary because retroactive interference occurs when you forget a previously learned task due to the learning of a new task.

16 When we store a new memory we also store retrieval cues and when we come to the same situation again, these retrieval cues can trigger the memory of the situation. Retrieval cues can be external/context cues in the environment, for example the smell of the place where the memory was formed, or internal/state cues such as the mood we were in when the memory was formed.

17 The students who were asked the leading question 'how fast were the cars going when they smashed into each other' stored the meaning of the word 'smashed' as a retrieval cue and 'smashed' implies something is broken. When the students were later asked whether they saw any broken glass, the word 'smashed' had created a false memory for breakage, so these students reported seeing broken glass.

18 The study by Loftus and Palmer was a laboratory experiment but Yuille and Cutshall was an experimental case study. The participants in Loftus and Palmer were students, but the participants in Yuille and Cutshall were mainly adult witnesses to a violent crime.

19 In a cognitive interview the police take care to reduce the anxiety felt by witnesses. They minimise distractions, avoid interruptions and allow the witness to take his or her time. The witness is encouraged to report every tiny detail of the event, recreate the context of the event, recall the event in different orders, and may be asked to recall the event imagining what someone in a different place might have seen. Recreating the context and imagining the event from a different perspective may provide contextual cues that help the witness remember the event.

20 Interactional synchrony is a special type of interaction between caregiver and infant that helps to develop and maintain attachment. Interactional synchrony may include reciprocity, in which a baby moves in time with the caregiver or where the caregiver smiles in response to the infant smile and/or imitation in which the baby imitates the facial expression of the caregiver.

21 Up to 3 months of age: indiscriminate attachments. The newborn is predisposed to attach to any human. After 4 months infants show a preference for certain people. Infants learn to distinguish primary and secondary caregivers but accept care from anyone. After 7 months most infants have a special preference for a single attachment figure. The baby looks to particular people for security, comfort and protection and shows unhappiness when separated from a special person. After 9 months most infants develop multiple attachments and become increasingly independent.

22 One surrogate mother was made of wire but dispensed milk so baby monkeys could get food from 'her', the other surrogate mother was covered in soft towelling cloth so baby monkeys could get comfort from 'her' but the cloth mother did not dispense milk to all the monkeys.

23 Imprinting appears to be innate and happens after birth (hatching) instantly, while attachment develops in stages. A baby gosling imprints on the first object it sees and 'recognises' this as its mother; a human infant learns to recognise its mother.

24 A child's bond with his or her caregiver can be explained in terms of learning and reinforcement, because the caregiver relieves the physical needs of hunger and thirst and the child learns to associate pleasure with the caregiver.

25 According to Bowlby, infants have an innate tendency to form an attachment and attachment takes place during a critical period or not at all. Thus, according to Bowlby, attachment is nature rather than nurture.

26 A securely attached infant shows some anxiety when the caregiver departs but is easily soothed, plays independently and greets the caregiver's return with enthusiasm. In insecure–avoidant attachment, the infant shows indifference when the caregiver leaves and at reunion the infant actively avoids contact with the caregiver. In insecure–resistant attachment the infant is distressed when the caregiver goes but when the caregiver returns the infant may resist contact and is not easily consoled.

27 Maternal privation is when a child has never been able to develop an attachment to his or her mother or another caregiver.

28 Adoptive parents put a lot of effort into relationships between themselves and their children but do not make special efforts to ensure good relationships between their children and peers.

29 Bowlby believed that an attachment creates an internal working model (a cognitive schema) that is a set of expectations for all future relationships and that this first attachment forms a template that gives the child a feel for what relationships are like. The internal working model is used in future years to develop other relationships and in determining parenting skills in later life. For Bowlby, a secure attachment as a child leads to emotional and social stability as an adult, whereas an insecure attachment is likely to lead to difficulties with later relationships and in parenting styles.

30 Abnormality as behaviour that deviates from the statistical norm *or* abnormality as behaviour that deviates from the social norm *or* abnormality as deviation from ideal mental health.

31 OCD. Freddie shows obsessive cleanliness — the compulsive behaviour of hand-washing and compulsive checking and rechecking that his hands are clean.

32 The two-process model of learning a phobia can explain Milly's phobia of spiders. Classical conditioning is involved because the fear of spiders is first learned by association and operant conditioning because as Milly avoids every fear-provoking stimulus (spiders) this prevents her from unlearning the fear, so operant conditioning explains why her phobia persists.

33 Systematic desensitisation is a behaviour therapy in which the person's phobia is broken down into small stimulus–response units. The patient is taught muscle relaxation and breathing exercises and then creates a fear hierarchy, starting at stimuli that create the least anxiety and building up in stages to fear-provoking images. Patients work their way up, starting at the least unpleasant and practising their relaxation technique as they go. The role of the therapist is to help the patient recognise the reason for the fear, and whether the fear is rational or not. The therapy consists of the construction of a hierarchy of fears, training in relaxation, graded exposure (in imagination) and relaxation and practice in real life.

34 The behavioural approach assumes that all behaviour is learned; that what has been learned can be unlearned; that abnormal behaviour is learned in the same way as normal behaviour.

35 The cognitive triad (see Figure 5 on page 55). Beck believes that depressed people get drawn into a negative pattern of viewing (1) themselves, (2) the world and (3) the future.

36 The cognitive approach to depression assumes that the human mind is like an information processor and that people can control how they select, store and think about information. In the cognitive approach, psychological problems are caused when people make incorrect inferences about themselves or others, and have negative thoughts about themselves and the future. For example, depressive people often believe that they are unloved, that they are failures as parents, and that nothing good will ever happen in the future.

37 OCD is an anxiety disorder. Anti-anxiety (anxiolytic) drugs such as benzodiazepines slow the activity of the central nervous system (CNS), reducing serotonin activity and thus anxiety, and increasing relaxation.

OR students may suggest:

Beta blockers act on the autonomic nervous system (ANS) to reduce activity in the ANS associated with anxiety — these drugs are effective because they reduce heart rate, blood pressure and levels of cortisol.

38 OCD may result from a deficiency of the neurotransmitter serotonin or a malfunction of its metabolism like blocked serotonin receptors.

Index

Note: **Bold** page numbers indicate glossary definitions.

Index